Shadows and Symbols

Shadows and Symbols

SERMONS FOR LENT AND EASTER

CARL L. JECH

SERIES C FIRST LESSON TEXTS FROM
THE COMMON (CONSENSUS) LECTIONARY

C.S.S. Publishing Company, Inc.
Lima, Ohio

SHADOWS AND SYMBOLS

5857 / ISBN 0-89536-751-3

PRINTED IN U.S.A.

Dedication

To Jeff and Dawn

Table of Contents

Part I. The Cross and Our Shadows

Part II. Surprising Symbols of Easter

Part I

The Cross And Our Shadows

The Cross And Our Shadows

Introduction

Many of us grew up singing the hymn "Beneath the Cross of Jesus" with it's memorable line: "I take, O cross, thy shadow for my abiding place . . ." This image of "the shadow of the cross" has been used in many different ways by poets and writers. In the hymn, it refers to a place of refuge and rest "from the burning of the noon-tide heat and the burdens of the day." The hymn also refers to the strength-giving character of the cross by comparing it to "the shadow of a *mighty rock* within a weary land." Surely the shadow of the mighty cross, like the "Mighty Fortress" of Martin Luther's hymn, has been a refuge and strength to Christians throughout the centuries!

But some have been critical of the way the cross hangs as a shadow over Christian people. They point to events like the Crusades, during which the shadow of the cross brought terror and violence to many people. Some would point to the burning of crosses on lawns or the smashing of windows in the homes of Russian Jews — using the cross as a battering ram! Others observe how some Christians seem to become almost masochistic and morose in their concentration on the suffering and death of Jesus.

The fact is that the word *shadow* often carries a negative connotation. We all know the happy song "Me and My Shadow, strolling down the avenue . . ." But more often than not the image is of murky shadows in contrast to light; people sneaking around in the shadows, up to no good; or, as we read in our text from the prophet Joel, "the day of the Lord . . . is near, a day of darkness and gloom, a day of clouds and thick darkness! Like blackness there is spread upon the mountains a great and powerful people . . ." It is not clear whether this "dark threat" is a reference to a plague of locusts, an enemy army, a dark and destructive "northeaster" (a terrible rainstorm) or some other disaster causing people to take stock of themselves and ask whether or not they really have their lives in order. The point is that a dark shadow looms over everyone and threatens to undo them!

1. Lent is a time to face some of the darker sides of reality

The famous psychologist Carl Jung emphasized that every person has a shadow side, a "not-so-nice side"to his or her personality, no matter how wonderful, selfless, "Christian" or loving he or she might appear outwardly. (Jung also had much to say about *dreams* as important indicators of what is really going on beneath the surface in our emotional and spiritual lives.) As Joel calls his people to "rend their hearts" and face their not-so-nice side in the wake of the Lord's judgment, so too Lent, calls us all to face up to the shadows in our lives. We are called to confront the sins and problems that cause pain and suffering for ourselves and for others, so that ultimately we might experience the mercy and grace of God to overcome them.

Joel 2:12-19 makes clear that confession and repentance are indeed good for the soul! One of the most beautiful, popular and encouraging solos in all sacred music is "If with all your hearts you truly seek me, you shall ever surely find me" from Mendelssohn's Oratorio *Elijah.* It begins by quoting these somber words: "Rend your hearts and not your garments. Return to the Lord, your God, for he is gracious and merciful, slow to anger . . . and repents of evil." We do not focus on shadows in order to wallow in misery, but in order to lighten — or even remove — shadows by shining the light of God's grace upon them!

2. Lent is a time to face criticisms that people make of the church

Is it true that Christians are a bunch of sour-faced purveyors of negativity and gloom? *Ash* Wednesday! Really! Who needs a religion that tells you to glorify *ashes?!* Perhaps the church has been guilty of the wrong kind of emphasis on sin and suffering. There were some shocking examples of this kind of preoccupation in Ken Russell's movie, *The Devils,* a story set in a medieval convent. There are those who in the name of Christ promote an overly negative preoccupation with sin, guilt, the evil things in the world. In the name of Christ they go on destructive "crusades" that harm other people. Is this the image we ourselves project to the world?

A trip to the dentist often is not particularly enjoyable (to put it mildly). But the alternative of ignoring what is causing a toothache or bleeding gums can be much worse. Even if a toothache subsides, it can flare up again at the most inconvenient moment! Lent *is* a little like a trip to the dentist. If we ignore what is wrong and never do anything but hope for the best, chances are the shadows will suddenly catch up with us and engulf us in darkness.

We dare not sweep sin under the rug. But neither dare we let sin keep us under it's heel! The interplay of lights and shadows in our lives is often subtle, as in any great work of art. The church can and should help us to deal with that subtle interplay.

Conclusion

The great theologian Reinhold Niebuhr was a progressive — one might even say liberal — thinker. But he said he could not, unfortunately, be a pacifist. His comment came in the time of the Second World War. His belief was that to be a pacifist was to deny the reality of sin and evil in the world. In other words, he believed that to refuse to stand up against evil when necessary would be not only cowardly, but more important, it would be *heresy!* It would be a failure to take seriously the Christian doctrine of Sin. It would be to make faith into nothing more than an escape from trouble. It would be to play the ostrich.

But we do not focus on sin in order to *glorify* sin. We do not face our shadows because we enjoy lingering in them. We focus on sin in order to overcome it. We face our shadows because doing so enhances our ability to experience joy, peace, love, understanding, hope and all the gifts of the Spirit.

As we gather around the Lord's table and as in the coming weeks we consider some of the painful realities — the shadows — in our lives, we need to remember that there is no victory without a struggle, that if we do not know how to feel pain then we will also not know how to feel joy, and that if we are afraid of our own shadows we will never have the courage to walk in the full light of day, in the full light of "the brightest and best *Son*" — Jesus Christ our Lord.

Look At Your Fixations!

The Shadow: Fixation

Introduction

In one of his classic comedy routines Victor Borge sits down at the piano and says to the audience: "Pardon my back. Pardon my *front*. . . But that's the way I'm built!"

Every coin has two sides. Our body has a front and a back. And every body casts a shadow. These facts are neither good nor bad in themselves. They are just facts of life. To say, with psychologist Carl Jung, that every person has a shadow side, a "not-so-nice" side to their personality, is not necessarily to make a negative judgment. The issue is not whether or not to have a shadow. The issue is how do we deal with our shadows. Three weeks from now, for example, we will take a look at *anger*. Now anger certainly can be a dark and evil thing . . . but *not necessarily!* The psalmist makes that clear when he says: "Be angry, but do not sin . . ." (Psalm 4:4). We cannot keep anger from casting its shadow over our lives, but we can do something about how we *handle* that anger.

Today our text brings to mind the phenomenon known in common parlance as a *fixation* or an *obsession*. The Israelites are reminded over and over again to fix their attention on the history of their liberation and their enjoyment of the promised land. The very name "Deuteronomy" highlights the "fixation" character of the Israelite preoccupation with the story of the Exodus, the giving of The Law and the entry into the promised land. Deutero means "second" (that which is *repeated)*. Nomos means "law." The book of Deuteronomy is a repetition, reaffirmation and reinterpretation of the old, old story of Moses and the deliverance from bondage.

1. Fixations can be good or bad

A lot depends on *what* our fixation is and *how* this fixation affects the rest of our life, our other interests and concerns. In 1975, Stanton Peele, a Harvard social psychologist, published a book titled *Love and Addiction.* His basic thesis was that there is no such thing as *physical* addiction. All addiction, he maintained, is a psychological matter of becoming so preoccupied with, so fixated on a particular facet of our experience that *all other interests* are blocked out. We literally develop a one-track mind, a myopic tunnel vision, that causes us to lose all perspective on the variety of relationships, experiences and concerns that should balance our lives. According to his definition, what many people call love is actually such a total fixation and dependance upon another person that the proper word for it is not love, but addiction!

Does this description cause twinges of discomfort in us? Is it possible that some of our most cherished concerns and relationships are actually the kinds of extreme fixations that amount to an addiction? Well, of course, it depends.

What or *who* is it that has possibly become a fixation for you? Is it your best friend's spouse? Is it alcohol? Some fixations are by definition neither good nor helpful. Like bad habits, some fixations are bad no matter how you look at them.

But perhaps the most common problem we face in the matter of fixations is *how* to know when a healthy concern or commitment has become an unhealthy preoccupation. How do we tread that thin line between love and addiction, between commitment and fanaticism, between our greatest strength and our greatest weakness. Yes, our greatest strength is often simultaneously our greatest weakness! Your devotion to the care of a sick loved one, for example, may be admirable, but your *unwillingness* to allow others to help you share the burden of that care may be destroying your health, your relationships with friends and other family members — in other words, your "selfless devotion" can indeed turn into a destructive fixation.

In the text from Deuteronomy this unique "nation" called Israel maintains a constant focus on and repetition of the history of its Exodus, its possession of "The Land" and its covenant of blessing with the Lord. Was this a good or a bad fixation? Hold that question in the back of your mind.

2. There are bad fixations

As we get older it often happens that some prominent feature of our body becomes even more prominent. A large nose becomes, it seems, even larger. Thin hair becomes even thinner. Personality characteristics and fixations, too, can begin to stick out much more noticeably as the years go by.

A visit to a convalescent hospital is likely to provide us with many examples of fixations that have totally taken over people's lives. There is the old man who wanders the halls and lounges day after day asking everyone in sight if they have a match or a cigarette. His mind seems unable to focus on virtually anything else. There is the woman who had to leave her native land in mid-life who now constantly asks everyone over and over again where they came from, what their nationality is. There are likely to be many poignant souls who constantly plead or demand "I want to go home!" (They have never been able to face the reality that this communal institution is their new home.)

I think also of the person who comes to the church office reiterating a tale of woe about being evicted unfairly by a landlord. It turns out this happened years ago and the person became so fixated on the injustice of the event that wandering from place to place trying to win sympathy and help has become a permanant lifestyle. When the Pope visited Canada, one newscast showed two young girls sobbing with intense emotion as "the Holy Father" touched and kissed them. Whether it is the Pope, Michael Jackson or the Beatles, how many people have gone through their life fixated on some kind of "he-touched-me" experience that colors their life forever?

Obviously, it makes quite a difference what our fixations are. Some seem by their very nature destructive. Others could be either good or bad depending on how they affect or are integrated into the rest of our life. The excitement of meeting the Pope could inspire a life of faith, service and devotion; or it could turn one into the kind of religious fanatic who, like some people I have met, "think religion" (or religious art, or music, or ________?) twenty-four hours a day. It was Martin Luther who said, "God is interested in a lot of things besides religion." The injustice of an unfair eviction could simply fixate one on "what a terrible victim I am." Or it could motivate a life of dedication to working against injustice to others — a life turned outward to others that gets one back into the mainstream.

To look at our destructive fixations or at our "bad memories" can be extremely beneficial for us. L. Ron Hubbard's Scientology/-Dianetics religion is based upon clearing the soul (or "Thetan"as he calls it) of "engrams" (bad memories and fixations) so that the mind can function more effectively. While it is easy to quarrel with Hubbard's theology, it is not difficult to understand the popular appeal of this "new religion" which is a kind of combination of science fiction and Freud. We all know that we have destructive fixations that we would be better off without. Even such a simple thing as the habit of always eating wheat grain breakfast cereal and never corn can be a fixation that keeps us from getting proper nutrition. Why always eat lima beans when there are at least sixty different varieties of beans from which to choose.

3. There are good fixations, too

One of the main characteristics of a great genius is that such a person becomes "fixated" on some interest, idea, talent or theme, and this interest shapes that person's entire life — usually from very early on. Mozart and Mendelssohn composed and performed music even when they were very small children. Bobby Lewis, the acting teacher who has taught such people as Henry ("the Fonz") Winkler, Meryl Streep, Karl Malden, Katherine Hepburn and many others, is fixated on the idea that *imagination* is the key to success as an actor. Everything he does as a teacher of the dramatic arts revolves around this theme of imagination. The poet W.H. Auden has written that the person who is a genius is most fortunate precisely because there is no doubt about what to do with one's life — the overriding talent is all-controlling and what the person *must* do is also what the person most *wants* to do.

We have good habits — such as getting regular exercise, worshiping, taking vacations, brushing our teeth, getting a good night's sleep — habits that somebody at some point might call an addiction or a fixation, but that we know are good for us. There isn't even anything necessarily wrong with being an "exercise nut." Certainly a fixation may limit other possibilities, but nobody can do everything and, as long as a habit is basically healthy, we can be quite free to pick our fixations. I am reminded of the old line: "I'm a fool for Christ . . . Whose fool are you?" An extreme commitment or dedication can be an important and necessary focal point in our lives!

Let us return to our text from Deuteronomy. Was the Israelite "fixation" on their liberation from bondage in Egypt and their inheritance of the promised land a *destructive* or a healthy fixation?

Even here, I think we have to say "it depends." There are some Jewish people who are so preoccupied with "The Land" (Zionism) or with *the holocaust* that they are virtually blind to the needs and the sufferings of other peoples. Instead of learning from their own oppression not to oppress others, they fixate on the injustice *they* have suffered and refuse to see the ways in which their current actions and attitudes may be oppressing *others.* Looking closer to home, there are unfortunately many Christians who are so morally self-righteous that in the name of promoting "traditional values" they trample all over other basic values like "liberty and justice for all."

Within the Christian tradition, we have sometimes accused each other of being fixated either on "good works" or on "grace alone." Putting too much stress on our "works" seems to leave God out of the picture, while emphasizing "salvation by grace alone" seems to render us so passive (some argue) that we give up caring what mere mortals think, believe, or do. The correct "fixation," of course, is to be aware of the *paradoxical sense* in which we are both passively dependant on God's grace and actively co-workers with God in making this world and our lives what God intends them to be.

The ultimate fixation pictured by our text is summed up in these words: "And you shall . . . worship before the Lord your God." (v. 10) Elsewhere it is expressed: "You shall love the Lord your God with all your heart, and with all your soul and with all your might." (Deuteronomy 6:4) Don't we have to admit that this sounds like the kind of extreme fixation that amounts to an addiction?

To look at or treat any of our *human* relationships in this way would indeed be the kind of "love" that Stanton Peele calls an addiction. No human being can *stand* to be *worshiped,* to have others depend totally and exclusively upon him or her for everything! Furthermore, it would not be fair for me to depend on someone else in this way. Only God is capable of bearing the burden of our total and absolute trust! Only God is always completely available to us in unconditional love and acceptance. Unconditional love is important in our close human relationships, but our best approaches to this love are limited. Even those who are closest to us and who care about us the most cannot be as close and dependable as God can be. Call it total commitment, call it love, call it an addiction, call it a fixation. Such an understanding of and relationship with *God* is beyond criticism! It puts our whole life in proper perspective. When we fix our eye on God alone, all other fixations are diminished. They lose their power to control or to destroy us. Then we can "rejoice in all the good that the Lord our God has given us."

Conclusion

Sometimes our fixations are part of our "darker side," our "not-so-nice" side, our shadow side. Maybe we should each ask ourselves what fixations we will exhibit in our old age that might cause others to look at us with pity, humor or admiration. Will my fixations reveal me to be a slave or a free person, a fanatic or a well-balanced and sensitive human being?

Will my eye be *fixed* on the loving God who is interested in a lot of things besides "religion"? *That* is certainly the fixation worth cultivating!

What Is All This Talk About "Inclusiveness"?

The Shadow: Exclusiveness

Introduction

The comic strip *Kudzu* by Doug Marlette features a bulbous-nosed preacher who wears a broad-brimmed hat something like the hats worn by Roman Catholic cardinals. In one of these cartoons the preacher says: "Our scripture lesson today is from the twenty third Psalm . . . 'The Lord is my therapist, I shall not experience negative feedback . . . He maketh me to mellow out in green pastures. He leadeth me beside Perrier waters . . . He gives me permission to get in touch with my feelings . . . He leadeth me in the paths of positive self-image . . . Yea though I walk through the valley of bad vibes, I won't get uptight . . . ' At which point he looks up, chagrined, thinking to himself 'I hate these modern translations!' "*

I really like seeing the preacher portrayed as a humorous, likeable, ordinary person, because often the image of "the preacher" is a rather negative one. "Sermon" and "missionary, more often than not, seem to have a bad connotation in our society. "Don't *preach* at me!" the daughter yells at her mother. "Take your *missionary attitude* and shove it in your ear!" the man yells in exasperation at the friend who has been pressuring him to take up jogging and vegetarianism.

Now, of course, it would be quite easy for me to defend sermons,

*(Jefferson Communications, Inc. distributed by Tribune Company Syndicate Inc.)

preachers, and missionaries. It is easy to give a lot of flimsy excuses why we don't like sermons, preachers or missionaries, and just as easy to expose the way in which we use these excuses to remain in our comfortable, self-centered ruts. But, sad to say, there are some ways in which the church . . . preachers . . . missionaries . . . are to blame for negative attitudes which many people have toward the church — and religion!

1. Some images of the church make it look like an exclusive club

There is a dark, dangerous, *shadow* side to some of the views Christians hold about the nature of the church. Some view the church as a "lifeboat" in which "a few lucky souls" can be saved from the sea of sin in which everyone else is drowning. Or we stress the "narrow way" which few find. Or we develop some form of "holier-than-thou" understanding of the way in which Christians are to be different from everybody else. After all, it is argued, doesn't the word "church" come from the Greek word "ekklesia" which means "called out"?

To a point all of these images or definitions of the church are good. But when we carry them too far, or in the wrong direction, there can be some unfortunate results. The church can slip into being an *exclusive club* in which the object is not to bring people in but to keep them out, not to rejoice in the variety of gifts and members in the body of Christ but to say "you can come in if you are *like us!* The task becomes not to shoulder our special *responsibility* to the rest of the world, but to brag about our special *priviledge* of being God's chosen people!

A recent letter to the editor of a major church journal gives a strong flavor of this exclusive attitude. The gist of that letter was something like this: I am sick and tired of all this business about "inclusiveness" in the church! I think the whole thing is an effort to destroy the church and its uniqueness and to let the "humanists" take over.

Other critics of the ubiquitous talk about "inclusive ministry" these days would remind us of the old adage which says that "those who stand for nothing will fall for anything." We must, they would insist, stress the ways in which Christians are different from all other people, that Christians are "called out of the world" into a separate fellowship, that the "requirements" of being a Christian and a member of the church mean that many people will be *included out!*

2. God's covenant with Abraham is remarkably inclusive

Before we take this theme of the exclusiveness of the church too far we need to remind ourselves that if the covenant made by God with Abraham was conceived in exclusive terms, *we would be included out!* In more ways than one, this story of how the Lord sealed a covenant with Abram by means of a smoking fire pot and a flaming torch passing between the two halves of three animals that had been cut in two, seems very far removed from our contemporary world. But even this ancient method of sealing an agreement is not as far removed from us as may at first appear. We today still talk about "*cutting* a deal." This contemporary figure of speech comes directly from this ancient practice of sealing an agreement or covenant by walking through or passing some object through the two halves of a sacrificial animal. We also realize that this ancient covenant between God and Abram is not so far removed from us when we remember the first time this covenant is described three chapters earlier, in Genesis 12. "By you all families of the earth shall bless themselves." (v. 3) God's purpose in making this covenant is to bless *all people.* When in today's text (Genesis 15) Abram is told that his "descendants" will be as numerous as the stars in the heavens, it seems clear that more than just his immediate Israelite descendants are included. Later, in his letter to the Romans, St. Paul uses this story of how Abraham "believed God and he reckoned it to him as righteousness" to show how the covenant made with Abraham is linked to the covenant made through Jesus Christ, a covenant intended to reach far beyond the limits of the original "children of Israel."

Two major problems stand out in relation to this covenant. First of all, it seems *impossible.* Abram and Sara are childless. The answer comes quickly and it is part of a pattern which we meet over and over again in the Bible: from small, insignificant and even seemingly impossible beginnings, God is able to do great things! God works often through the most unlikely "heroes." Abram will lose his faith many times only to have it continually restored and to become known as the "father" or ultimate exemplar of faith. (Hebrews 2) Still today, God continues to accomplish great things through unlikely people, through people who appear at least to be outside the church. I think, for example, of some great playwrights or composers.

The second problem with the covenant is perhaps best expressed by means of the joke which I have heard some present-day Jewish comedians tell with obvious relish: "I have heard, Lord, this thing that we are supposed to be your chosen people. Considering our history, I got one request: choose someone else!" The concepts of the "chosen people" and of "the promised land" have been controversial and problematic ones in the history of Israel. The point we need to see is that, both with the original Israel and with the "new Israel" (the church), it is an overly exclusive understanding of the chosenness and of the promise that leads to trouble!

In both the old and the new covenant, the chosenness is more in terms of special *responsibility* than in terms of special *privilege.* We are chosen to *share* with the world the wonderful news and promise of God's grace and love for "all the families of the earth." If Jews or Christians are chosen and different just for the sake of being chosen or different, what is the point? But if *they* are special so that *every person* can come to see that they too are special and important in God's eyes, then the point is that "God is Love!"

As long as the problem of Israel and the Palestinian State today is defined in terms of who can have *exclusive* rights to land and governance, then resolving the "Middle East" question will probably remain impossible. But if the issue is defined in terms of how people can *share* the land and the promise of peace, then there is hope! As long as we stress who is excluded, there will be trouble. When we stress how everyone can be *included,* then there can be peace.

3. God's Covenant through Jesus is absolutely inclusive

What then is the mission and the message of the church? Is it to define carefully who the "heathen" are and then to *keep them out?* Is it to make certain that everyone who joins the church is "like us" — same doctrine, same priorities, same race, same political leanings, same lifestyle?

Frequently in his public lectures, the late psychologist and author Erich Fromm described five stages along the way to becoming a truly loving person. At stage one, he would say, I only like myself. At stage two I like myself and anyone who is *like me.* At stage three I like myself, people who are like me and people who are part of my *group.* Stage four means that I like myself, people like me, my group and other groups that are like my group. Only at stage five has one truly "arrived," said Fromm. The "stage five person" doesn't just like those who are like himself or herself. The stage five person *loves.* The stage five person *loves everybody!* Fromm, whose personal tradition was Jewish, said that it is hard to find good examples of "stage five" people, but that Jesus was certainly one.

It is not our calling as Christians, as members of the church, to make everybody *just like us,* to make everyone fit the same mold. *Some* of the differences between the various Christian denominations are a healthy reflection of the way in which the church is a "cradle of diversity," as Dr. Nelson Trout (the first black man to be elected a bishop in the American Lutheran Church) described it. (*Lutheran Standard,* No. 4, 1983) I like the point of view which speaks not of the Lutheran, Baptist or Roman Catholic *church,* but of the Lutheran, Baptist or Roman Catholic *movement* within the Christian Church. When we fight and differ over who "really believes," over who is and is not saved, then we are in danger of misunderstanding our mission and our message. It is not our job to make everyone just like us; the Church — our congregation included! — can and should include people of diverse doctrinal perspectives, races, lifestyles, cultures, political beliefs and philosophies, many more than it does at this point in history. In the strictest sense, it is not our task to "make everyone Christian." Our calling is *to share the grace shown us in Christ and to let God be the judge of the results of that sharing!*

Conclusion

In his most famous Christmas sermon, Martin Luther made a rather sobering observation. "You say that if you had been there when Jesus was born, you would have welcomed him — not like the innkeeper and others who had 'no room.' Would you really? I don't think so." It is a sobering thought that if it were up to us, we perhaps would not include the likes of Abraham, Moses, John the Baptizer or Jesus in our church — Moses who had committed murder, Abraham with his multiple wives, John the Baptizer with his wild hair and strange diet, Jesus with his unusual lifestyle and questionable parentage. In the name of "standing for something" will we stumble over Jesus? In the name of a narrow-minded "morality'' will we exclude everyone who refuses to become ''like us?''

Let our ''missionary style'' be a relaxed *sharing* of the grace of God revealed in Jesus, the Christ. Let us focus on whom needs to hear this message and *feel* this message in the way we relate to them. Let us focus on who needs to be *included* and not on whom we can keep out. And let us allow God to be the judge of the results of our ''missionary work,'' our preaching, our *sharing*. Our shadow side wants to judge, to ''keep the bad guys out,'' to control everything. But the cross comes to banish these shadowy desires. We live in the New Covenant: ''Behold, I bring you good tidings of great joy, which shall be to all people.''

That's God talking about inclusiveness!

Excuse Me!

The Shadow: Low Self-Esteem

Introduction

One of the most popular programs in the history of old time radio was *The Shadow*. "The Shadow" was the alias used by fictional crime-fighter Lamont Cranston. A creaking door introduced each show, followed by the sinister and now-famous words: "Who knows what evil lurks in the hearts of men? The Shadow knows!" then came a sinister laugh. (The preacher might risk an imitation.)

Have you noticed that the Bible does not seek to cover up the darker side of even its greatest heroes? In his textbook on World Religions, John Hutchison writes: "(With) 'biblical realism' . . . there is little or no glorification of a hero, as in Greek epics, but the plain-spoken narrative of plain men, in all their strength and weakness, all their good and evil, in short, in all their poignant humanity." The writers of the Bible confront head-on the shadows that lurk in the hearts of all of us. They pictured the many ways in which we miss the mark of being what we were intended to be and they called it *Sin*. To understand Sin is to realize that our negative self-image is often justified. Our lives *are* full of dark shadows.

1. Moses said "Excuse me!" from going to Pharaoh

Looking at the full story before us in chapters three and four of Exodus, we see the great Moses suffering from low self-esteem. "Who am I that I should go to Pharaoh?" he protests. "What name or authority can I call upon that can possibly impress him? What can I *do* to impress him? I am not eloquent . . . I am slow of speech and tongue.'' Moses doesn't mention it here, but the reader remembers that not long before this famous incident at the burning bush, Moses also had *killed* an Egyptian in a fit of anger. Even his fellow Hebrews had criticized him for being a murderer, and Pharaoh had ordered the death penalty for Moses! Now the Lord wants *him* to be the special messenger and agent of the Hebrew's liberation from Egyptian bondage? ''Who? Me? You've got to be kidding!'' And so, the excuses fly. Excuse me! ''Oh, my Lord, send I pray, some other person.'' (Exodus 4:13)

Moses was all too aware of the evil that lurked both in himself and in Pharaoh — and in the whole situation. This knowledge was paralyzing him into inaction.

Now there is some danger in ''psychologizing'' — in drawing a psychological portrait from a story which is more interested in theology and faith than it is in psychology. But in this case there is indeed a close and obvious correlation between theology and psychology. God wants us to be honest with ourselves, to confess our sins, our shadows. But God does not want us to despair and withdraw as a result of this psychological honesty, this theological confession of our sinfulness. What if Moses had never found the courage and restored self-esteem that allowed him to face Pharaoh and demand ''Let my people go!''?

2. We bark ''Excuse Me!'' to mask our anger

Comedian, Steve Martin, is known for the retort ''Well Excuuuuuuuuuuuse me!'' The expression as he uses it contains a strong element of angry defensiveness. He is saying in effect, ''Excuse me for livin', but you aren't so perfect yourself!'' I may be ''unworthy,'' but you are just as unworthy.

People who are extremely critical of others usually are betraying the fact that they do not like *themselves!* This is an easily missed fact of life, but one which also becomes obvious when it is pointed out. The person, who is secure and comfortable with himself or herself does not need to or will not be bothered to spend time criticizing and tearing down others in order to look better by comparison. There are too many *positive* things to be done, to waste time ''knocking'' others and their efforts. I am speaking here of the kind of compulsive and constant carping criticism that earns the complainer the reputation of "sourpuss" or worse! Lodging occasional complaints against your brother or sister or spouse, or roommate or fellow worker does not necessarily mean that *you* have a bad self-image. Legitimate criticism, both positive and negative, can be expressed from a position of strength and high self-esteem. But excessive negativity is almost always a warning sign. If I feel good about myself, I don't need to make a snide remark to the golfer who accidentally hits my ball instead of his own; I don't need to get all worked up over the waiter whose service wasn't up to the standards I expected; I don't need to gossip about the way other parents handle their kids.

When we encounter the chronic complainer or excuse maker we frequently find ourselves thinking "What's *her* problem?" When I am confronted with an unkind or cutting remark that I feel I don't deserve, instead of barking back, I try to take the attitude which says "That's *his* problem." The chances are that truer words could not be spoken.

The young, insecure, confused Moses' approach to an offending Egyptian was to kill him. We could say that this act was both a cause of and an effect of his poor self-esteem. The older, wiser Moses was more interested in building "his People" *up* than in tearing the Egyptians *down.* Jesus said that when we love ourselves, then we are strong enough to love even our enemies.

In his film *Crimes of Passion,* eccentric British director Ken Russell presents us with a caricature of a priest/minister (it's not clear which) one who is riddled with self-hate and self-doubt over his sexuality. He is so tortured with conflicts that in the end his self-image is literally stabbed to death. The picture reminds us that we must make an important distinction between low self-esteem that is *deserved* and low self-esteem that is based on a *faulty premise.* This guilt-ridden preacher in Russell's movie has internalized the false notion that sex is sinful. The fact is, of course, that only *bad, destructive sex* is sinful. There is an organized movement today within the Roman Catholic Church to challenge the church to develop a more complex understanding of the role of sexuality and pleasure in the lives of a complex variety of individuals. It may well be that unless this challenge is met by all churches, the church will become shockingly irrelevant to the lives of more and more people. In his book *Embodiment,* James Nelson* laments that a tendency toward

*Professor of Christian Ethics at United Theological Seminary, New Brighton, Minnesota.

anti-bodily, over-spiritualized attitudes toward sexuality have led to a situation in which "many people have left the church to seek the wholeness of their sexual humanity elsewhere." When we express our sexuality in irresponsible ways that hurt and abuse other people, then indeed we deserve the feelings of low self-esteem that *will result.* At such times we have sinned and we need to pray for forgiveness. But many people have been led to feel low self-esteem and self-hatred over aspects of their sexuality that may not be sinful or destructive at all! To some degree, modern psychology and medicine have been helpful in allowing us to better understand which kinds of sexuality are harmful and which are not. The point here is that sometimes our low self-esteem is based on mistaken and misguided expectations! What we need may not be forgiveness, but education!

But what about the bad self-image which is *not* based on a *mistake?* What about the low self-esteem that is richly deserved because of our very real sinfulness?

Only the light of the cross of the Lord of grace, the Christ, is bright enough to wipe out the shadows which we legitmately should wish to banish from our lives. When we try to excuse or forgive *ourselves* we are never quite convinced that our self-image has been washed clean. But when we know in faith that *God* has cleaned up our image, then we know that we can stand tall with no apologies.

3. God excuses us when we abandon all excuses

Precisely when we abandon our excuses which try to patch up our self-image, precisely *then,* God is ready to excuse us! Now we must understand that the word "excuse" does not mean to effortlessly let someone off the hook as if there were nothing to it. The harmful results of our sins — the disabled child injured through another person's carelessness, for example — may linger on indefinitely. The story of the cross of Jesus shows us that it costs God dearly to forgive us. The word *excuse* means simply "to cause something to go out." In this case, God causes our sins to "go out," to go away from us. When we are excused or forgiven by God the point is *not* that we have been "let off the hook," but that we have been given another chance to improve. We have been given a clean slate in order that we might *go out* and begin again to be what God intends us to be! It means that the good image of God in us can never be entirely erased!

Last week we chuckled at the paraphrase of the 23rd Psalm which includes the line "The Lord is my therapist . . . He leadeth me in the path of positive self-image." As humorous as this contemporary language can sound, there is also a strong element of truth in this version of the psalmist's reflections. To walk with God is to remember that we are, after all, made in the *image* of God, the God who is the source of all goodness.

In some Christian churches the prayer appointed for this day includes these words: "Help us to hear your Word and obey it, so that we become instruments of your redeeming love; through your son, Jesus Christ our Lord . . ." How can we be "instruments of God's redeeming love" if we do not *like ourselves?* If we don't like and love *ourselves* we can hardly be effective ambassadors of God's redeeming grace. We can also make this same point in a backwards sort of way: the most dangerous walking "time-bomb" in the world is a person who hates himself or herself! Such persons do not feel good about life, do not respect life — their own or anyone else's. One of the most common ingredients in low self-esteem is the feeling that one is not loved, not accepted and loved unconditionally simply because of one's own intrinsic value as a human being. A person who feels this way often fails to learn how to relate to another person in a relationship for the sake of the value of that relationship alone. Even the most intimate relationships are made into some kind of "business deal" in which one is always calculating by asking "What am I getting out of this?"

The gospel message of God's unconditional, redeeming love for us is the fundamental basis for a high self-esteem in which we value ourselves and others for our own sakes alone, without any "calculation" of advantages and disadvantages.

For the first few months of her life, Helen Keller was an average baby. Then disease took away her sight and her hearing. By the time Anne Sullivan arrived to be her teacher Helen was like an animal. This child was often dubbed "the phantom" because of the way she hovered around the family home. Through the miracle of incredible patience, love and devotion, Anne Sullivan was able to break through to human communication with Helen, to give her a self-image, *and* self-respect — a sense of worth and value as a human person. To know the story of Helen Keller is to know what it means to move from a non-existent, shattered or negative self-image to a wonderful awareness of ourselves as beautiful creations of God. To be reminded of her story is to be reminded that we can look through and beyond the evil in our lives, the shadows in our lives, the sin in our lives, to the glorious possibilities that are inherent in our status as children of God, the God whose name, as revealed in the dramatic episode at the burning bush, is best translated as "I will be What I will be." To come into a living relationship with *this* God, the God of all being and becoming, is the ultimate in "possibility thinking!"

Conclusion

Just as Moses was in many respects the father of God's people, Israel, even so the author of that earliest Gospel, Mark, was the first one to capture the message about Jesus: Evil demons *do* lurk in our hearts, but God is stronger. Pain, evil and suffering do lurk in the shadows, but God is in the center of things! The shadows are peripheral. With God's help, we can face our shadows and keep them from getting the upper hand. We can have a positive self-image.

One of my favorite ways of remembering the importance and beauty of a positive self-image is to repeat the story of the small black child who responded to bigoted taunts by shouting back: "What you say about me isn't true, because God made me, and *God don't make junk!"* That's a line we would all do well to apply to ourselves. Made in the image of God, we have sinned and become like junk. Our shadows threaten to engulf us. But God in grace has redeemed us, has bought us back from the junk heap through the cross and resurrection of Jesus, and restored our original beauty and goodness. Rather than saying that we are excused from fulfilling God's great expectations for us because we aren't worth much, God excuses us in a way that restores our worth, our self-esteem, and reminds us that *God doesn't make junk!*

Hold Me When I'm Angry

The Shadow: Anger

Introduction

Why was *All In the Family* such a popular television program? I suspect it was because the "love-hate" relationships between Archie, Mike, Gloria and Edith helped us better to understand the ways in which our love is mixed with anger, our joys are mixed with pain, and our laughter is tinged with sadness and pathos. Even longsuffering Edith with her good-natured naivete could get angry. Who can forget the time when *she* tells *Archie* to *"stiffle!"?* Or the episode where Archie accuses her of being a saint, of not being human, and Edith, hurt and angry, cries out "I am too human! I'm just as human as you are! I got feelin's just like everybody!" I think also of the time that Archie and Mike are locked in a cold storage room and Mike comes to see Archie in a much more sympathetic light.

We all have a hard time dealing with the fact that we inevitably hurt, become angry with, yes, even sometimes *hate* the ones we love! We have heard the old saying that the opposite of love is not hate but indifference — but we still are bothered when we feel angry or resentful toward those we love and care about.

The people who followed Moses out of Egypt experienced their own version of *All In the Family*. God's little family, Israel, displayed very mixed feelings about the Manna that had fed them during their wanderings in the wilderness. At first they are full of love and thankfulness toward God for the miracle of this manna — thought by some modern scholars to be the honeydew excretions of scale insects, plant lice and other insects . . . secretions which rapidly turn into drops of sticky solids in the dry desert air. But in the book of Numbers, chapter eleven, verse six they begin to complain bitterly that "there is nothing at all but this manna to look at." In reaction to this fickle love-hate attitude on the part of his children, we read that "the anger of the Lord blazed hotly." (v. 10) Now, in our text for today, we read that the days of "reproach", of *disgrace* for Israel are over. They enter the promised land. The manna ceases and they eat again the varied produce of the land. The suffering, the anger, the disgrace are "rolled back" (that's what the name *Gilgal* means), and in place of *dis*grace there is now *grace* and *peace* in the family of Israel again.

1. Anger Must Not Be Kept In The Shadows

During this Lenten season we are talking about "the cross and our shadows." Today as we consider the end of the long-running story of Israel's experience with the manna in the wilderness, I believe we are confronted with the issue of *anger.* How are we to understand the wrath, the anger, the *dis*grace which seems to be as much a part of God's nature as is love and grace? How can we cope with our own mixed feelings of love and anger toward each other and toward God? How are we to comprehend the tension between the Cross as *grace* and the Cross as *disgrace?*

In a sense, the real question before us is whether or not it is even correct to think of anger as a part of the shadow side of life! Mental health experts tell us that *repressed* anger, *denial* of anger is one of the most common and destructive problems we all face! To give an extreme example, a recent book about People's Temple leader Jim Jones,* tells us that repressed anger toward his parents for what he felt was their neglect of him as a child was an extremely important factor in Jones' ultimate disintegration. The authors of this book see a definite connection between the death of his mother and the tragedy at Jonestown a few months later.

The collective wisdom of our mental health experts is that we need to learn appropriate ways in which to express our anger. But the psalmist also understood this. In Psalm 4 we read "Be angry, but sin not." (v. 4) And the message is repeated in the letter to the Ephesians (4:26) "Be angry but do not sin; do not let the sun go

---

*(Raven: The Untold Story of the Reverend Jim Jones and His People, Dutton, 1984)

down on your anger." Clearly, the question seems to be not how we can avoid being angry, but how we can properly express our anger. We might say that the main way in which anger casts a shadow over our lives is the way in which *bottled up* anger explodes in countless indirect and destructive forms of behavior. Once again we can learn from the example of Anne Sullivan and Helen Keller. Anne was able to teach Helen that she no longer had to break things in order to show that she was angry. Once she learned the meaning of words, Helen could *say* she was angry!

Should we never *control* our anger? The November 1982 issue of *Psychology Today* magazine featured a cover story on this question. The conclusion of the article was that people who too easily give in to every irritation with an outburst of anger accomplish little more than "raising the noise level of their lives." Ventilating anger is helpful, the author, Carol Tavris, suggested, only when it restores control and reduces a feeling of powerlessness."

I like to make a distinction between being honest and outspoken in a healthy, mature sense; and being outspoken in a childish manner. There is a huge difference between refreshing honesty about our anger and childish tantrums. I think of the organist who would childishly vent her spleen by playing hymns much too slowly or much too fast. As congregation, pastors and organists, we should expect to rub each other the wrong way once in a while. We need to expect some hostility once in a while and prepare ourselves to deal with it as a natural part of a dynamic process and relationship. It is precisely because we sometimes try too hard always to be "nice" and agreeable that we are confronted with the irony of that old line, "There's no fight like a church fight." Even within the family of the church we need to learn to "fight fair" — to be constructively honest about our differences and the things that get under our skin. Sometimes that may mean knowing when it won't do any good to bring a particular grievance out into the open, but more often than not I think it will mean that we can facilitate what is called "conflict utilization" — not the "management" of conflict, but the kind of open-ended give and take that leads to growth. (To speak of *managing* conflict is to expect more control of ourselves and of the situation than is either possible or desirable.)

Frederick Buechner warns against one clearly *destructive* way of expressing anger. He suggests that anger is a deadly sin when it takes the form of licking our wounds, of savoring the prospect of bitter confrontation, of returning pain for pain, of smacking our lips over grievances long past. To become basically "an angry person" is to be of all people most miserable. When lovers quarrel, amazing growth can take place. But when "haters" quarrel, the results are disastrous. Some ways of being angry do cast dark shadows.

Along similar lines, Lewis Smedes, who teaches at Fuller Theological Seminary in southern California, warns against the destructiveness in the kind of anger that seeks revenge, that seeks to "get even." In his 1984 book, *Forgive and Forget* (Harper and Row), Smedes explains how letting go of this kind of anger by means of forgiveness is both spiritually and psychologically healthy for us. More often than not, when we have been terribly hurt by someone, our unique pain or loss is such that truly "getting even" is impossible. When Pope John Paul, for example, forgave the man who shot him, he was not able to undo the consequences of the man's actions, but for his own part at least the Pope was able to avoid letting what had happened to him become a permanent hangup that could sour the rest of his life. There are many situations in which forgiveness is the only effective and appropriate alternative to anger. If we think we benefit from letting our anger eat away at us, says Buechner, we will be shocked to discover that *we* are the skeleton at the feast!

2. It's What We Do With Our Anger That Counts

None of us can avoid being angry. As Luther said, "We can't keep the birds from flying over our heads, but we can keep them from building a nest in our hair." We can't avoid becoming angry, but we can control what we *do* with our anger!

Sometimes we can see our anger as a *gift*. The television show *Highway to Heaven* once included an episode about a young man who had lost his legs in a motorcycle accident. Angry and bitter, in the hospital he lashed out at those who tried to help him, including the young woman who loved him. Then, suddenly, during one encounter the anger turned to tears and now, instead of bearing the brunt of his anger, the young woman achieved the kind of tender closeness she had hoped for.

Dr. Elizabeth Kubler-Ross, the famous authority on death and dying, tells us that we should consider it a compliment when a dying person shares his or her anger with us. It seems absurd at first when we are told to be grateful that a person is lashing out at us when we are "innocent," but if we realize that the dying person is *trusting* us with her deepest feelings, we can indeed look upon this sharing as a great honor. Following through on this insight, Dr. Ross adds that it is even okay to be angry at God, because "God can take it! It is part of God's *job* to deal with our anger!" Our willingness to give and receive anger can be a great gift. It can show that we care.

Rabbi Harold Kushner, in his bestselling book *When Bad Things Happen To Good People,* suggests that, rather than being angry *at* God for the suffering and injustice in the world, we should understand ourselves as being angry *together with God* at this suffering and injustice. Righteous indignation, he contends, is a gift from God. It is God, he says, who gives us our sense of what is fair or unfair. Our feeling of compassion for the afflicted is a reflection of the compassion God feels in response to suffering. God's anger works through us when we respond to life's unfairness with sympathy and positive action.

Of course, sometimes our righteous indignation can be misguided or misplaced. It may have been psychologically healthy for the Israelites to express their tremendous anger toward the Babylonians in Psalm 137 — "Happy shall be he who takes your babies and dashes them against the rock!" — but in the light of later developments "righteous indignation" can come to look ridiculous. The frustration of the wilderness wanderers with "nothing but this manna to eat" was understandable, but in the light of the later developments recounted in our text for today when they begin to occupy the promised land, the petulant complaining about the manna which helped them to reach their goal becomes something of an embarrassment. When the reproach or disgrace of the Wilderness or of Babylon is past, the realization sets in that the line between blessing and curse is often a thin one. The manna and the captivity may have seemed at times like a curse and a cause for anger. But in many ways and in the long run both were also blessings! (You may remember too that, when the Israelites pounced greedily on the quail that looked like an alternative to the manna, a plague resulted that almost wiped them out.) Often we need to recognize that a situation is ambiguous, that it is not all black and white — and this realization can temper our anger.

Sometimes our anger needs to be *redirected.* Instead of being angry at a person who has hurt us, or being angry at God, we should direct our anger at the *situation,* at the *disease,* at the *personality characteristic* that annoys us. The cross of Jesus reflects God's *anger* toward *sin* but his *love* toward *people!*

When the subject of the disease called AIDS is discussed, some people become angry at the heterosexual Africans with whom the virus appears to have originated. Others become angry with homosexuals or drug users. But the real focus of our anger should be on the virus itself, the disease itself — not on the victims of the disease! I trust that all of us who are parents know the difference between telling a child that his or her *behavior* is bad and telling a child "You are bad." I trust we make it a habit to say "What you are doing makes me angry, but, of course that doesn't change my love for you as a person."

Another way to redirect anger is to take the *energy* generated by our anger and apply it in a deliberate way to some positive end. The church as an institution has done something that hurt you or someone you care about? Don't quit the church! Have a lover's quarrel with it. Work to change or improve those things in the institution that offend you. If your quarrel is with an individual person, learn to combine your statement of how the person has angered you with a statement of the good things he or she does that you appreciate.

The major problem with most "redirected" anger is that the redirecting is done unconsciously. We *deny* the existence of our anger only to have it surface elsewhere, in ways that are totally inappropriate and often destructive. Tardiness, sloppiness, sullenness, are often indirect expressions of anger. The files of psychiatrists are no doubt full of examples of ways in which the lives of countless people have been thrown out of joint by an inability to deal directly with anger. Anger over an injustice suffered can become a lifelong hostility to all forms of authority, causing endless difficulties for the person whose repressed anger makes him into an extreme "individualist." All it may take to avoid this trap is to learn when and how to say "This makes me angry!" Admitting anger is the necessary prerequisite for overcoming anger.

Conclusion

The world is full of angry people. Often it is not clear that anger is their problem. I think of one couple that broke up because one person in the relationship had a whole collection of unpleasant personality characteristics as a result of repressed anger and low self-esteem. The way in which this person's anger was always bubbling just beneath the surface made it virtually impossible for intimacy and warmth to occur. Here was a person who was angry and didn't know it.

I think, on the other hand, of the couple in which the wife responded to virtually every difficult situation with nothing but anger. The husband wanted to be held and comforted, but all the wife could do was fuss and fume. The husband also was angry about some of the things that had happened in their life, but he knew that there was something more important than the anger. His message to his wife was "hold me when I'm angry." But she was so busy with her anger that she was seemingly blind to the possibility of a positive response. The marriage ended in divorce. Their version of *All In the Family* was canceled.

God knows we get angry. But as God made a covenant with the Children of Israel, his "Family," and held on to them even when they were angry, so God holds us even when we are angry. "Be angry, but do not sin." May our attitude toward one another be: Hold Me When I'm Angry. May our prayer to God at the foot of the cross be the same — "Hold Me When I'm Angry."

Afraid of Salvation?

The Shadow: Fear

Introduction

We are all familiar with "The Seven Last Words of Christ." But somewhere along the way, some inventive soul came up with a different version of the seven last words. "The Seven Last Words of the Church: "We Never Did It That Way Before!"

Clearly, this little "zinger" is intended to warn us against the dangers of becoming set in our ways. The point is that our *fear* of change, our *fear* of something new, our refusal to adapt, could lead to extinction. The church could stop being what God intends it to be.

"Be Not Afraid" is one of the most oft-repeated admonitions in all of Scripture. There are many ways in which the shadow of fear casts a pall over our lives. Probably our greatest fear is the fear of being left alone. How many College Choirs have performed Bach's great motet "Be Not Afraid; I Am With Thee"? The theme of "Emmanuel," God *with us,* is the ultimate answer to all our fears. One of our major goals in these next few minutes will be to come to a better understanding of the relationship between our fear of "the new thing" and our fear of being left alone.

1. Don't Be Afraid of God's "New Thing"

The second half of the Book of Isaiah which begins at chapter 40 speaks more explicitly of salvation and redemption than perhaps any other portion of the Old Testament. Here in chapter 43 salvation is connected with the "new thing" that God is doing.

"Remember not the former things, nor consider the things of old. Behold, I am doing a new thing; now it springs forth, do you not perceive it?" (vv. 18-19) For the people who have been captive in Babylon, salvation brings a "new twist." By definition, salvation seems to include the element of "the new twist," the "surprise." And the issue is not perhaps so much whether we "perceive" it or not, but whether we are *afraid* to perceive it. Could it be that because it brings something new, we are actually *afraid of salvation?*

One famous interpretation of the story of the lame man who had been waiting for over thirty years at the pool of Bethzatha for someone to put him in the pool at just the right moment (John 5), suggests that the man's real problem might have been his *fear of being healed.* He had become so accustomed to his invalid status that the prospect of having to rise up and stand on his own two feet was not something he really wanted any more. According to this interpretation of the story, Jesus shocks him out of his lethargy and says in effect, "If you *really* want to be healed, you can have what you want this instant. Forget the pool. It has become an excuse. Decide! Make a change in your life. Don't be afraid of it!" Is it not true that in many, many ways we do indeed perceive the possibility of salvation, of healing, but that we are afraid of the changes it will mean in our life? We are afraid of being saved! We are comfortable enough with the way things are.

Perhaps a better title for this sermon would have been "Spring Forward Or Fall Back." This little saying that helps us all remember how daylight savings time works also expresses a more profound truth. That truth is that we are either moving, springing, forward or falling back. There is no standing still. Any of us who have taken lessons in some sport or art know this very well. Stop practicing, stop learning and you don't even maintain the status quo; you actually go backwards. Isaiah here describes God's salvation as a "new thing" that "springs forth." In the thrilling opening words of this portion of Isaiah the message "Comfort, comfort ye my people" is *not* the message that says you can rest now and stand still. No. The voice cries out, "Comfort, comfort . . . We're going to *move!* Let's get on the highway!" When God comes to love and save and free us, there is a lot of change, a lot of movement.

Now, of course, salvation does not mean simply change for the sake of change. Not all change is for the better. Not all change brings healing. We all appreciate the line in the hymn "Abide With Me" which reads "Change and decay in all around I see; oh, Thou Who changest not, abide with me." But we must not forget that the image of decay and change is also one of the primary symbols for the *resurrection!* The image of the seed that "dies" in the earth but springs forth with new life reminds us that "being changed" need not necessarily be a frightening experience. What *does not* change is God's love for us. The message of salvation is that God's love is constant and unchanging. But *that* unchanging love *does take many forms.* God's unchanging love removes our fear of the exciting changes that accompany salvation.

2. Don't Be Afraid of Growth

For those church bodies that practice Confirmation, this rite is not understood as a challenge to remain unchangingly set in ones ways. The person being confirmed is admonished to "*grow* in grace." A firm faith is not afraid of growing pains. Instruction in the Christian Faith cannot simply mean the learning of a set of doctrines, a collection of comfortable cliches. On one level, slogans or cliches are *inadequate* because every such truism has its opposite number. "Haste makes waste" *but* "a stitch in time saves nine." "One picture is worth a thousand words" *but* "looks can be deceiving." "Better safe than sorry" but "nothing ventured, nothing gained." "He who hesitates is lost" *but* "look before you leap." We say "Sticks and stones may break my bones while words can never hurt me," *but* we also speak of "adding insult to injury." On another level, slogans or cliches are problematic because they present us with profound paradoxes which force us to think deeply about the matter at hand. Luther wrote, for example, both that "Faith is a free gift from God" of which we are totally passive recipients, and yet also that "Faith is a good work, the greatest good work that a person can do." Ignatius Loyola, the founder of the Jesuits, tried to express this same paradox in his dual admonition: "Pray and trust God as if everything depends on God; *but* work and do your best as if everything depends on you." The point is that becoming involved in God's saving activity means that we will find ourselves thinking, reinterpreting, growing, changing. We will find ourselves struggling with the process of learning what it means to be "saved."

Another paradoxical or ironic realization that can help us deal with our fear of change, is the realization that in a variety of ways *we must change in order to stay the same.* No sooner had the "Where's the beef?" commercials made Clara Peller a household name than the advertisers discontinued and then changed the commercial. They knew that in order for the commercial to continue it's effectiveness it would have to be changed. Take clothing styles. If your goal in dressing yourself is consistently to avoid sticking out like a sore thumb, you will make it a point, within reason, to change with the times. If you desire to "stay the same," that is, to be a part of the mainstream of clothing styles, you will change with the times. To stand still when things around you are changing is to change! If evangelism is to remain effective in the rapidly changing world of today, we are going to need more than merely cosmetic changes in the way we apply the message of God's saving grace to contemporary life. A Christian congregation that wants to grow *wants* to *change!* It is not a denial of the gospel to change and grow in grace. It is a *fulfillment* of the gospel.

3. Don't Be Afraid of Christ

The many places in the Bible that speak of God making things new should make it clear to us that there are dangers in making *changelessness* or *absoluteness* the main ingredients in our concept of God. God's *love* and *grace* shown us in Christ clearly do not change. But what that grace means for us is another story — is *many* other stories!

After all, the entire Christian faith is based on a *reinterpretation* of the Jewish concept of the Messiah. The title, "Christ", is a Greek translation of "Messiah" which means simply "the anointed one." To say that Jesus is "the Christ" and that as "Christ" he does not change, can be simple for us on the level of faith. But on a theological level the matter is far from simple. We can pray to the Jesus Christ whose love does not change, and yet also discuss the *concept* of "Christ" that has changed and is changing in every generation. Theologians call this "Christology," and the very fact that it remains the most discussed subject in our seminaries is a major part of what it means to be "Christ-centered."

The message which tells us that Jesus is Lord and Savior is the message that tells us "God is stronger than evil." We are reminding ourselves today that *one* of the things this message of salvation does for us is to calm our fears. Besides our fear of change and of that which is new, Isaiah in our text also refers to our fear of the forces of nature ("the mighty waters"), our fear of enemies (war — "armies and warrior"), and our fear of the many forms in which we can find ourselves stranded in the "wilderness." Some of these fears may be perfectly legitimate. But to know the saving power of God is to have what it takes to cope with our fears. God releases us from the paralyzing power of our fears and sins.

Besides calming a great variety of our fears, the good news of God's love can also bring a surprising *variety* of changes. To a person who has lived a dissolute and chaotic life, the gospel might bring with it a stabilizing influence. To a person whose life is overly rigid and confined, the same gospel might bring a refreshing relaxation of inhibitions. "What Christ means to me or to you" might be a "new thing" every day. *Conversion,* as salvation is sometimes called, will make us less self-centered, but it will also help us *love ourselves* in the proper way.

In part, our fear of change is really the fear that life is not as simple as we would like to think. Pierre Teilhard de Chardin, the Jesuit scientist, suggested that in addition to thinking of God as *beyond us,* we should also visualize God as being *ahead of us* in the ongoing development of the creation. The God of creation and redemption, of creation and *re*creation, challenges us courageously to embrace those positive changes that bring us into the future. Instead of being always afraid of change and judging every "new twist" as bad, we need to perceive those "new things" that are coming from God.

After all, one of the most moving affirmations of the resurrection in the New Testament, 1 Corinthians 15:51, pictures change as God's ultimate gift: "Lo! I tell you a mystery. We shall not all sleep, but we shall all be *changed!*" Earlier in this same letter to the Corinthians, Paul refers to Isaiah (64:4 and 65:17), pointing out that the "new thing" which God has in store for his loved ones is beyond what we can either see, hear or imagine! Even as we pass through the valley of the shadow of death and change, God says to you and to me "Fear not. I am with you!" To be afraid of change could actually be to be afraid . . . of *Christ!*

Conclusion

Why and how do we become lonely? Doesn't loneliness happen when we are afraid to reach out in new ways to new people and relationships? We're afraid of being rejected, so we don't ask for the date. Our spouse or a dear friend dies, and we can't muster the courage to make changes and build new relationships. We try to stick with the comfortable, old ways, with nothing but our memories, and we find ourselves alone. We are afraid to meet someone we have never met, or to do something we have never done before. God reaches out to us in the bondage caused by our fears, our fixations, and all the other shadows which haunt us, and creates "a new thing," a new relationship. Likewise, let us reach out to God and to others. Old relationships may change and new relationships develop, but the sharing, the meaning, the love that these relationships bring into our lives never changes. God's salvation changes all our relationships — but for the better! Don't be afraid of salvation, and you will never be alone.

Christ Is THE ANSWER!

The Shadow: Arrogance

Introduction

I find it interesting that so many bathroom graffiti are religious in nature. I once noticed some graffiti in which someone had written "Christ Is the Answer." Underneath that, someone else had scrawled "What Is the Question?" And next to that yet another "artist" had scratched "Who Cares?"

My guess is that the person who wrote "Who Cares?" is someone who has had some kind of negative experience with religion, with the church, with people who call themselves Christians. It seems likely that in this particular case, the person was expressing a cynical reaction to a type of "Christian proclamation" that sounds more like arrogant boasting than like thoughtful sharing. The shadow side of our desire to share the gospel of Jesus Christ is that we can all too easily and all too subtly fall into the trap of displaying a "holier-than-thou" attitude which actually turns people off. The gospel is indeed a powerful message. But we must never forget St. Paul's continual warnings that we must at all costs avoid the temptation to *boast*: "By grace are you saved, through faith; and this is not your own doing, it is the gift of God — not because of works, lest anyone should boast." (Ephesians 2:8-9) Or again, Romans 3:27: "Then what becomes of our boasting? It is excluded."

We speak during this lenten season of "glorying in the cross." But obviously this is a profoundly unusual form of "boasting." Most of us have heard the joke about the fellow who is "proud of his humility?" The gospel of God's love for sinners is a message that makes us humble. Our ultimate dependence upon God's grace rules out any pride or boasting on our part. *And then,* we are given the tricky and risky and, I think we might even say, paradoxical job of proclaiming "Christ as the Answer" in such a way that we avoid any and all traces of "holier-than-thou" boasting! This mission calls for great sensitivity!

1. Christ is THE ANSWER to THE QUESTION

We are gathered here because we believe that Christ is indeed THE ANSWER. But first of all, we must understand what we *are* and *are not* saying when we share this claim. The shadow side of the people who waved palm branches on this day many years ago, is that they were expecting the wrong kind of answers from Jesus — and when they failed to see the kind of Messiah, the kind of Christ, the kind of ANSWER Jesus was, the shouts of "Hosanna" turned to shouts of "crucify!"

It is helpful to see the theme of this sermon in print because THE ANSWER is written in all upper-case (capital) letters. Our fundamental point today is that Christ is THE ANSWER to THE QUESTION, but not the automatic answer (small *a*) to all the questions (small *q*).

One of the most important principles in education is that the ability to ask good questions, the right questions, is just as important as the capacity for giving good answers. Isaiah, in our text, shows that he understands what the right question is, what the basic *human* question is. That question, as he phrases it, is this: *How can we be sustained when we are weary?* "The Lord God has taught me . . . that I may sustain with a word him that is weary." (v. 1) When we look to God, we are looking for an *ultimate* answer to an *ultimate* question. That question has to do with how we can keep faith, hope and love, and the will to live, in the face of even the most severe suffering, panic or despair. THE ANSWER is *the Grace of God* which sustains us no matter what. Isaiah was aware of that grace and in Christ it has become even more real to *us*.

Let's focus on a few brief examples of what God's saving grace means.

(1) We work as hard as anyone to do the will of God, to do "our best," to be good citizens of our community and of the world — to *do good works*. But what the grace of God does is to give us the proper *attitude* toward our efforts, as St. Paul said, to "work harder than them all." You see, we all know deep down that even our very best, when we manage to do it, is not going to be good enough.

We can't seem to make ourselves or our world perfect. Realizing this, we could easily give in to despair or complacency. Or we could become the type-A person who pushes himself or herself into a heart attack by simply trying too hard. The beauty of God's grace is that it keeps our motivation high and yet at the same time keeps us from taking ourselves too seriously. The secret of good living and the secret of the gospel, is having an attitude which teaches us both to struggle and to relax at the same time. Knowing that the world is ultimately "in God's hands" gives us the proper attitude toward the sense in which "God has no hands but our hands."

(2) Another way to say this would be to describe how a person who basks in God's grace can combine a sense of *urgency* with a sense of *humor!* What a "grace" it is to always keep one's sense of humor no matter what troubles beset us! Not that we naively "laugh off" our problems, but that we keep that sense of the broader perspective which inevitably leads to better coping with difficulties. To maintain "good humor" in this sense, is not the same as simply "having a joke for every occasion."

(3) Another helpful way to explain what it means to be "saved by grace" is to use the surprising image of what some have called "religionless Christianity." Although this phrase can be taken to mean a number of things, I take it to mean that the gospel of God's love and grace in Jesus Christ frees us from worrying about our eternal destiny. We can say, in effect, "my salvation and the salvation of the world is God's worry, God's business, not mine! What a relief! The ultimate answers are in God's hands, God's *gracious* hands, and what a wonderful message to share! It's not up to me to know or to decide who can and cannot be 'saved.' Here is a religious message that frees me from 'religious fears.' Now I have the proper frame of mind in which to go about living my life the best way I know how."

(4) Isaiah clearly shows in our text today that to be taught by God is not necessarily to have all the answers nailed down. In terms of the debate about the "inerrancy" or "infallibility" of Scripture, we need to understand that the Word of God "inerrantly" and "infallibly" *accomplishes its purpose* of sustaining us in our weariness, of bringing us God's grace in Christ; but this is not to say that every detail in the Bible is accurate, that the authors weren't affected by their particular, limited world views. THE WORD brings us THE ANSWER in the sense that the central message of Scripture is

sufficient to bring us faith, hope and love. The Bible is inerrant and infallible *in its ability to convey to us the gospel of God's saving grace in Jesus Christ.*

2. THE ANSWER helps us live with all the questions

Most importantly, we must become clear that Christ is the ultimate ANSWER precisely because his Grace gives us sufficient security and certainty to face the insecurity, uncertainty, ambiguity, adversity and lack of pat answers which are an inescapable part of life.

"Security," one famous aphorism says, "depends not so much on how much you *have* but on how much you can *do without.*" The secure Christian — secure in God's grace — does not need to have all the answers! Isaiah does not expect God to keep all of his "adversaries" away. "Who is my adversary? Let him come near to me." (v. 8) Having THE ANSWER does not make us immune to all troubles, does not give us pat answers to all questions, does not require us to keep all our questions hidden in the shadows. I had a good laugh recently when, right below a Billy Graham "My Answer" column in the newspaper there appeared a separate brief article with the headline: "Trying to Have All Answers Unhealthy." In the article, a theologian/psychologist warned against the mindset that cannot live with unanswered questions.

In the gospel of Mark we encounter what is sometimes referred to as the "Messianic Secret." One explanation of Mark's picture of Jesus as always discouraging people from calling him the Christ, has to do with Jesus' desire not to be misunderstood. Popular notions of the day had made the idea of "Messiah" into a panacea. People thought of the Messiah (the Christ) as one who would miraculously, gloriously bring the end to all troubles and the answers to all questions. Only the Centurian at the foot of the cross, who says "Surely this was the Son of God," is not rebuked for making a great claim about Jesus. Many New Testament scholars point out how this emphasizes Mark's point that Jesus is not the kind of panacea-Christ we tend to expect. Jesus is the Messiah more in the spirit of the Suffering Servant whom Isaiah pictures in the chapters from which our text for today is taken.

A Messiah who suffers with and for people, a Messiah who does not hide his face from shame and spitting, who does not shun the cross — Jesus is the Messiah, the Christ, who becomes most real to us precisely when we, along with the Centurian, see him *on the cross!* Surely, the kind of *Answer* God is giving us is something other than we might expect! Beyond naive "possibility thinking" or simple optimism, Jesus is the Christ who never makes us pretend that our sins, our suffering and our questions aren't as serious as they are! Christ is THE ANSWER precisely because none of the *terrible truths* about us and our world are powerful enough to separate us from "the love of God which is in Christ Jesus our Lord." The strange beauty of the cross is that it represents God's ultimate victory over the worst possible adversaries. It is THE ANSWER because it means that we never need despair.

Professor Arthur McGill gave a marvelous lecture at Harvard Divinity School in 1973, in which he drove home the point that the main purpose of the Gospel is to help us face our pervasive *neediness.* In contrast to "a gospel of *having*" he eloquently described how the Gospel of Jesus Christ enables us to face a constant flow of "needs that cannot be satisfied, destructive circumstances that cannot be controlled." What Answer do we receive through Jesus? What do we learn, morning by morning, from Christ? "We learn courage and endurance to bear needs, and in need learn how to receive and how to give, learn how not to be overthrown by unforseen disaster."

We learn the daily process of receiving God's grace — something which is totally different from having all the spiritual or material resources, having all the easy answers. We help and share with others not out of a sense of superiority and with pity, but out of a sense of our common, human neediness. Just as the manna in the wilderness could only be received anew each morning, so too we cannot *have* or *possess* all spiritual resources on a permanant basis.

To quote McGill again: "We cannot seek to have available ahead of time, within our control or ownership, whatever we may require for every contingency — money in the bank, water in the reservoir, blood plasma in the hospital, and expertise at the other end of the telephone." No. We learn from the Cross how to *struggle* with personal crises, with ethical values and issues, with economic and political concerns. We learn that although it is all right to take some thought for the morrow, we can't predict what tomorrow will bring. I wonder if, when he gave the lecture, this Harvard Professor who was only in his early forties, knew that he was soon to die from a rare disease. How prophetic his words were in his own life! How can there be a glib or easy answer when the brilliant career of a young theologian is snuffed out?

All of this is to say that as Christians we must be particularly wary of the shadow of spiritual arrogance. For Christ to be our ultimate ANSWER, does not mean for us to *have* all the answers. In fact, the reverse is the case. Our relationship with Christ gives us humility and makes us even more sensitive to the difficult questions and challenges that we all face.

The mother of the famous DeBolt family, that California family that has adopted so many special and disabled children, reflected the spirit of this humility on the Phil Donahue show she refused to brag about the fact that none of their twenty children has had any serious drug-abuse problems. She said she only takes one day at a time and thanks the Lord that, so far, her kids have not been sidetracked with drugs. If anyone could brag about her family it is this woman, but she refuses to be arrogant. It is a beautiful quality and, paradoxically, it is in large part precisely *because* she doesn't take it for granted that her family is above such troubles that, I suspect, the children *will not* become victims of drugs.

Conclusion

The comedians Cheech and Chong have used this line: "I used to be all messed up on drugs, but now since I've met the Lord, I'm all messed up on the Lord."

We must not fall into the trap of using Christ like a panacea drug, expecting a Messiah who will insulate us from all pain and give us all the answers, making us like robots who don't have to think and struggle for ourselves. It is *not* better to be "hooked" on Jesus than to be "hooked" on drugs. It is not good to be "hooked" on anything! Christ doesn't "hook" us. Christ *forgives* us and *frees* us from guilt so that we can each day go out and have another chance to struggle with all the challenges and questions that life brings. Christ is THE ANSWER who helps us live *WITH* all our questions and needs.

Love Can Be Hard Work

The Shadow: Laziness

Introduction

Tonight I'd like to begin by sharing with you an idea I have for a short screenplay. In scene one, Mr. & Mrs. Church attend an evangelism committee meeting in which they are trained to call on "unchurched, prospective members." They are reminded of Jesus' *command* in Matthew 28 to "make disciples of all nations." The next scene shows them making a call on a single-parent mother with three small children, one of whom seems to be what might be called hyperactive. Scene three finds this new family visiting a communion service, but as the young mother responds to the *command* of Jesus that she "eat and drink in remembrance of me", her children cause a slight commotion. In successive scenes as time goes by this young mother is subjected to a number of complaints, both to her face and behind her back regarding the behavior of her children in church services. But no one offers to help her or befriends the children! The final scene shows an empty church pew and smug worshipers glad to be rid of the disturbances. They have forgotten the primary *command* of Jesus — that we *love one another!*

1. Love cannot be commanded

On one level, love cannot be commanded. Love in this sense refers to that inner feeling by which we warmly *desire* to do something or to relate to someone without any external constraints forcing us. When Jeremiah speaks of a "new covenant" that will be "written on the heart" he is describing a situation in which people do God's will not because they are forced or commanded to do it, but because they want to do it. From this point of view, love is an emotion, a feeling, which cannot be forced, manufactured or created by an act of willpower. Law is a matter of piety, not legalism.

The "new covenant" theme as picked up by Jesus and his followers is a new *kind* of covenant in just this sense: We no longer relate to God in terms of meeting the requirements of the law, but rather we freely endeavor to do God's will precisely because God in grace has removed all "requirements." In gratitude for God's "saving grace" we can now view all our efforts to do our best and please God as inadequate but acceptable *responses* to God's forgiving love.

The problem with viewing love only as an emotional state of desire, however, is that our emotions, our feelings, are fickle! Our emotions are shadowy, volatile and unpredictable. The *shadow of laziness* often daunts our love. We need to be reminded that love is also hard work and that, as such, it *is* appropriate to speak of love as something which can be *commanded.*

2. Love **can** *be commanded*

The word "Maundy" is related to "mandate." It means "command." Today is "Command Thursday." In the Gospel of John we read: "A new commandment I give to you, that you love one another as I have loved you." To *command* love is to realize that our desires and feelings must be undergirded by determination and effort. We can desire to reach the "unchurched," but if we bring people in without being sensitive to their needs, our "lazy love" probably will not amount to much. Love is not just a sentimental feeling. Love is an act. Love is an act of caring and sharing. Folk singer Pete Seeger has said that in his opinion "share" is actually a better word than "love" because it is more specific, more descriptive of what loving action is all about. To love is to become involved in serious and sometimes unsettling debate and action on important social issues. To love is to share our vulnerability and neediness with one another, giving and receiving help. To love is to volunteer. The list of possibilities is endless: Red Cross, United Way agencies and projects, meals-on-wheels. Recently I was made aware of the need for volunteer receptionists at a local Community College in the Older

Adult Education program.

Not all the loving work that needs to be done is necessarily enjoyable. We cannot be commanded to *like* a person, for example. But love goes deeper than mere liking, and, therefore, we can be commanded to *love.* God does not expect us necessarily to like our neighbor, but God does expect us to *love* our neighbor! The unique kind of love with which Christ loves the church is what St. Paul calls *agape.* Agape love is that kind of love which loves the unlovable, the outcast, the person who doesn't seem to deserve love. The beauty of this kind of love is that it teaches us to "*love* even those whom we don't *like*"*!* Or, to put it a little differently, it helps our love to stay alive when people we usually like aren't at their best, when they aren't being particularly lovable. There is an organization designed to support the parents of "difficult" or disturbed children called "Tough Love." The philosophy of this group is that a very deliberate firmness is often what troubled children need. Being "tough" shows that someone cares. Every couple that gets married needs to be reminded that the ability to continue loving one's partner, even when that spouse is not at his or her lovable best, is just as important if not more important than erotic attraction. To be able to face conflict within a congregation, a family, a business, a community — to be able to deal with conflict without falling apart — that is what love, real love is all about. I like the adage: "Love is what you have been through together."

Jeremiah says that those living in the new covenant will "know the Lord." The image of God "writing on their hearts" attests to the heart as something more than the seat of the *emotions.* Those who know the Lord in this way will internalize not just the *desire* to follow the law of love but also the *will* and *determination* to follow the law of love. They will understand themselves as being under a *command* to love.

3. Whatever motivates it, love will always be personal

Whether our love is a spontaneous, emotional response or a conscious, determined effort, *as love* it will always be *personal.* The story of Jesus is central for us because, as the Christ, Jesus personifies love. The expression of our faith in the form of a meal, the Communion, the Lord's Supper, is wonderfully in keeping with this *personal* nature of love. To be a part of the church is not primarily a matter of joining an institution or accepting a set of doctrines. It is above all being part of a close-knit, caring *community!* We take the time and make the effort to listen to one another's stories. We consciously set aside time to discover and develop *intimacy.* We recognize that studying and listening to sermons may not change our basic personalities, but we trust that by becoming aware of the forces that mold us we can counteract those shadows which negatively affect our behavior. We trust God to be with us, to relate to both our strengths and our weaknesses.

One of the better recent movies about real love is the picture about the young high school football player who was counting on his football ability to get him out of his small town and into the possibility of an engineering career. The movie was called *All The Right Moves.* This title clearly did *not* mean that the characters in the story always did the right, best or loving thing. The coach was too sensitive to criticism. The young athlete was hot-tempered and self-centered. They both had their own way of always needing to think that they were right, and it was exactly this stubbornness that brought them to loggerheads. Eventually the coach kicked the young man off the team and the rest of the movie portrays how they hurt and, finally, helped one another. The young man's girlfriend helped by opening lines of communication with the coach's wife. The young man himself tried many ways to reconcile with the coach. Finally, in a surprise ending, the coach not only admitted his stubborn mistake but offered the young man a place on the big college team to which he was moving.

As I see it, the title of this movie has a number of levels of meaning. "All the Right Moves" refers to the talents of the two main characters both of whom know how to *move* on the football field. It refers to their somewhat arrogant tendency to think that they always make the right *moves.* It also refers to their discovery that admitting to one's mistakes and sins and shadows is the "rightest" *move* of all. In this film, the characters all struggle, grow, learn from their mistakes and learn to communicate. In other words, they learn to practice *love.*

Conclusion

Whether we think of the command to "make disciples," or to share the "Lord's Supper," or "to love one another," the important thing is that we make a commitment to care, share and grow with one another. We won't always make the right moves. But if we truly work at loving each other, we will be a part of God's "new covenant." We will not lay ourselves open to the charge that our love is lazy. We will banish the shadow of laziness and people "will know we are Christians by our love."

The Dramatic Shadow of Death

The Shadow: Despair

Introduction

On Ash Wednesday we began this series on *The Cross and Our Shadows,* by asking whether we Christians have an unwholesome *preoccupation* with evil, sin and suffering. Surely that question comes home to us most dramatically on this day when we would hold up the cross of Jesus for all to see! If you have seen film director John Huston's movie *The Bible,* you had the theme of Genesis 6:5 drummed into your ears: "The Lord saw that the wickedness of man was great in the earth, and that every imagination of the thoughts of his heart was only evil continually." The message and the film made for great drama.

In contrast to this emphasis, a great deal of religious and other literature holds up the idea that all evil is but a shadow, an illusion. I was once asked to conduct a memorial service for a woman who had been loosely associated with Christian Science, the group founded by Mary Baker Eddy. The family asked me to stress that death itself is only a shadow, that it isn't truly real. They wanted me to be sure to quote the 23rd Psalm: "Yea, though I walk through the valley of the *shadow* of death . . ." Let's not dwell on death, evil and pain, they pleaded. To some degree I was able to go along with their request. But not without some uneasiness.

1. Death Is Real

The message of Good Friday is that death is *painfully real* and that it cannot be smoothed over, romanticized or ignored. As a reference to the nation of Israel as a whole, our text from the "Suffering Servant" poems of Isaiah refers to the heavy burden of special responsibility placed upon God's Chosen People. The history of Israel is the dramatic history of the *painful* struggle for righteousness and peace on the earth.

As a reference to a special group within Israel, or to Isaiah himself, these words about being rejected — full of sorrows and grief — indicate that the road to wholeness and health requires that griefs be borne and sorrows carried! And above all, as a reference to the cross of Jesus, the description of a person "marred, beyond human semblance" drives home the awful reality of suffering and death. Not only does death rob Jesus of his Divine form, it also robs him *even of his humanity!* A more dramatic confrontation with the *dark side* of reality could not be imagined! The stark reality and terror of *anyone's death* is made clear when we use Isaiah's words to describe even God's only begotten Son as "pouring out his soul to death."

To face the grim reality of the "grim reaper" is to confront *despair* in its ultimate form. Ironically, the great quantity of violence and death on the TV screen, for example, does not necessarily help us to understand death and despair. People are "bumped off" so casually and frequently for the sake of television "drama" that death seems to become almost a game. My own observation is that an NBC "After School Special" about the despair of a high school student trying to cope with a seriously retarded brother living at home, does a better job of portraying how people are pushed to the breaking point, than do the "action/adventure" dramas. The boy is teased by schoolmates. The time that should go toward studying is spent "babysitting." When he finally does get an assignment done, his brother pastes it full of labels from food cans in the kitchen. The viewer of such a program gets to see what big words like iniquity, despair and oppression are really all about on a very personal level in an everyday context.

Anthropologist Margaret Mead liked to describe us human beings as "homo *saps,*" because although "homo sapient" means "the wise one," we so often exhibit negative and self-destructive behavior. And then, to top it off, we *deny* these darker sides of our nature. We *pretend* that evil is an illusion. We kid ourselves that our problems aren't serious. We immerse ourselves in silly diversions.

In his famous theological classic, *Christus Victor (Christ the Victor), Gustav Aulen of Sweden, describes Good Friday as the day on which the Christ looked straight into the face of the devil. The ultimate confrontation between good and evil, life and death, is taking place, and it is a terrifying conflict, a soul-shaking drama.*

2. "Shadows" Are Real

Now, it is true that we believe Christ to be the Victor over sin, evil, and death. But in order to understand the dimensions of this victory, we must see that the "shadows" over which God prevails are themselves very real! All the shadows we have been dealing with in these last weeks and all the evils that plague mankind are not just "in our heads." Fear, anger, laziness, compulsions, bigotry, arrogance — these are words that describe concrete, real, human behavior which has concrete results. The final form of despair leads to death and death makes us desperate. Our very attempts to convince ourselves that death is "only a shadow," only a simple transformation, only a form of "sleep," that death is not as bad as it seems — these attempts themselves demonstrate the awful reality of death. If it weren't so terrible, we wouldn't work so hard to deny it.

Perhaps it might be more accurate to say that, as Christians, we have a profound *ambivalence* regarding death. In light of the Resurrection message we *can* say with St. Paul that we would "rather depart and be with Christ." In the stories of the raising of Jairus' daughter and of Lazarus, Jesus himself speaks of them as being not dead, but "asleep." Yes, death casts a terribly dark shadow, but the light of God's Son ultimately eliminates this shadow. As Christians, we have more reason than anyone else to believe that death has lost its sting, that death need not be feared.

And yet, as Christians who can never forget the terrible sufferings and death of Jesus on the cross, we also have more reason than anyone else to know that death is a terrible *enemy!* The "shadow of death" is indeed a most terrifying enemy — a source of the most profound pain that we as human beings can experience. In the earliest gospel account of the crucifixion, The Gospel of Mark, Jesus is pictured as dying in despair, crying out "My God, my God, why have you forsaken me?" It is not until the writers of Matthew, Luke and John have had more time to assimilate the full impact of the meaning of the life and death and resurrection of Jesus that their accounts of the crucifixion balance out the horror of Good Friday with the assurance that Good Friday is the beginning of something good and not simply "the bitter end." It is in *their* accounts, written considerably later than Mark, that the picture of Jesus' death includes the more confident words such as "Today, you shall be with me in paradise" and "Father, into your hands I commend my spirit."

The cartoon character, Charlie Brown, is associated with the phrase "Good Grief." This expression, which is also the title of an excellent little book by pastoral counselor Granger Westberg, was perhaps most effectively explained by Schultz in one of his Sunday *Peanuts* offerings a few years ago: Lucy is feeling sad and Charlie Brown is trying to cheer her up. He offers to do things for her and to bring her things but when he says "Is there anything I haven't thought of?" Lucy responds "Yes, there's one thing that you haven't thought of . . . I don't want to feel better!" She screams it so loud that Charlie is knocked upside down.

The worst thing we can do is to say or do things that make it *seem* that we do not really take seriously how terrible other people feel! It may be *true,* for example, to say to a grieving person "You'll get over it in time." But more often than not it is *not* appropriate to say that, because the real message being conveyed is that I don't really and fully empathize with how terrible the sufferer feels. In fact, perhaps the most important and helpful thing you can say to a person experiencing profound grief is this: "I know I can't possibly know how bad you feel, but I want you to know how much I care about you."

People must be allowed to feel bad when they *need* to feel bad! Grief can be good for us. Which of us would dare go to Jesus on the cross, Jesus who is feeling forsaken by God, Jesus who is (depending on the version of the creed you prefer) "tasting death to the full" or "descending into hell," and say to him: "There, there now, it isn't as bad as all that"?

Another way of talking about being "acquainted with grief" would be to take note of what many experts say about the gruesome element in many fairy tales for children (like those of the appropriately-named Grimm brothers). I think the experts are correct who conclude that, when the witch is pushed into the oven or when the wolf eats grandma, children are being taught to cope with the reality that bad things happen to us. One writer on the subject suggests that the reason people like horror stories is because we know "that something bad is going to happen to us" and scary stories prepare us to cope with the eventual bad things that do indeed happen to us. These stories become a way of "rehearsing" for our own times of trial and grief. According to this point of view, it is a mistake to censor all frightening elements out of children's stories. This is not to say, of course, that we should *dwell* on violence and negativity.

It is never too soon to learn that pain, evil, suffering and death are real and that we must all learn to face them and cope. Understanding the dark, the shadow side of reality is as important as looking on the bright side. To do so is not to be preoccupied with sin and evil but to be *in touch* with the whole of reality. And "being in touch with reality," by the way, is one basic definition of mental health. It is also a factor in *spiritual* health!

3. Death Is Really Defeated

It is not easy to live with our Christian ambivalence about death, to live with the dual awareness that *death is real,* but that death is also *really defeated.* One way to do this is to follow Matthew Fox and his writings on spirituality. Fox stresses the idea that if we can't experience pain then we also cannot experience joy. Life, by definition, cannot always be the proverbial bed of roses, he insists. And he is right.

Another important way of living with our Christian ambivalence about death is to exercise our sense of humor. Put in a stock of cemetery and funeral jokes. Develop at least some appreciation for satire and black humor. I like the series of Charlie Brown "kick-the-football" jokes where Lucy cons Charlie into attempting to kick the stuffings out of the football with such lines as "young people have to have faith and trust," and then when Charlie falls flat on his back, having been betrayed by Lucy who *again* pulls the football away just as he tries to kick it, Lucy beams and says: "That's what I like to see — young people with faith and trust!" Even much of the current "punk" phenomenon is a form of this kind of "black humor." To *pretend* to *celebrate* death, evil and negative things can be a tongue-in-cheek way of having the last laugh on sin and death.

And, of course, the fundamental way in which we "live through" our ambivalence about death is to project our own deaths vicariously onto Jesus. The message of Isaiah in our text and of the Good

Friday story is that we alone do not bear the full burden of our sins, of evil, of suffering, of death. The image of "God taking our place," of God making himself an offering for sin, of God bearing for us what we cannot bear — this image of the *vicarious* sufferings and death of Jesus, the Christ, is the image that ultimately makes it possible for us both to face sin and death and yet keep our distance from sin and death. To use the words of poet Dylan Thomas, we can both "rage against the dying of the light (death)" *and* "go gentle into that good night" (also death). Death is a real enemy. But it is a *defeated* enemy.

Conclusion

Do you know what words first inspired Handel to write his *Messiah?* They were the words from our text: "He was despised and rejected . . . a man of sorrows and acquainted with grief." Handel had suffered a stroke and his career as a composer had fizzled. When the offer to pay him for a sacred oratorio first arrived, he rejected it. But he could relate to these words about suffering and grief! He composed the music for these texts first. They expressed well his own despair. It was only *after* he had faced his shadows, his despair and pain, that he was able to compose his dramatic and glorious "Hallelujah Chorus."

Part II

Surprising Symbols of Easter

The Butterfly Rock

Introduction

Do you know what your name means? Many names do have a definite historical or linguistic meaning. Jeffrey, for example, means "peaceful." Helga means "holy." Vivian means "full of life." Carl means "strong" or "manly." Michael means "one who is like God." You would be surprised at how many names have religious or biblical background. All the various forms of the name John go back to the biblical, Hebrew name Jo-nathan — the *Jo* refers to *God* (Jehovah or Yahweh) and *Nathan* means gift. Thus Joan, Joanne, John and other related names all mean "gift from God." Most dictionaries have a place in the back where you can look up the meaning and background of your name.

The popularity of various names seems to go in cycles. For a while there are a lot of Bills and Johns and then during another period of time there are a lot of Chris's or Shauns. Words like Grace, Hope and Faith were popular as names for girls at one time. As I look around, it also seems that there is a noticeable trend in the naming of new congregations being formed today. Names that reflect the meaning of Easter appear to have grown in popularity: Resurrection; Christ the Victor; Lord of Life; Cross and Crown. These names which emphasize *love of life* and the *continual renewal of life* could well be long overdue symbols for and reminders of the upbeat nature of Christian faith.

In our text for today, Peter preaches an Easter sermon. He tells his audience that his good news is not for one group of people only but for everyone. He explains how in the story of Jesus we learn of God's victory over evil and we learn how forgiveness makes us overcome judgment and face life with renewed zest. But in this case, the real Easter message is the preacher himself — Peter. He had been given this new name by Jesus (his original name was Simon) but it has taken quite a while and some profound experiences for the *meaning* of his new name to sink in! The name *Peter* means "the rock," but for most of his time as a disciple of Jesus, Peter had been anything but a rock. He had been fearful and insecure. When the chips were down, he denied he even *knew* Jesus. In the book of Acts we finally see Simon transformed into Peter. How appropriate that perhaps the most famous church in the world, St. Peter's in Rome, is named after this transformed disciple of Jesus.

1. A Cocoon Is A Great Place To Be From

The story of the Resurrection is not so much a story about the empty tomb as about *changed lives.* In recent years, the butterfly has become an increasingly popular symbol for the Resurrection. The emergence of the butterfly from its cocoon, its "metamorphosis" from a worm into a beautiful, delicate flying representative of spring, is a most appropriate metaphor for the Easter message of new life. "Metamorphosis" means to "change form" or "to be transformed." That's what the Resurrection is all about, and that is what happened to Simon Peter! Fearful, insecure, unreliable Simon emerged from his cocoon to become Peter, the Rock. Like a butterfly he has undergone a metamorphosis. Peter is *"the Butterfly Rock!"* What a surprising and yet appropriate symbol for Easter! As actor John Houseman would say, Simon started out as *mush,* but he came out of his cocoon transformed into a solid *rock,* a bold proclaimer of God's good news — the gospel.

The turned-upside-down life of the apostle Peter is an example of what Marshall McLuhan meant when he said "the medium is the message." This transformed disciple of Jesus, this "butterfly rock," is himself living proof of the reality of the Resurrection. Something has happened that has given him a new vision and understanding of life. The tradition/legend which says that Peter finally was crucified *upside down* because he didn't feel worthy to die in the same way as his Lord may be more symbol than fact. But it is an intriguing symbol. Peter's perspective on life had truly been turned upside down by his encounter with Jesus. In the cocoon of his former life he had been afraid of imprisonment and death. In Acts we meet a Peter who is no longer afraid of prison and death and faces both, ultimately, with confidence (this word confidence literally means "with faith"). When Peter "opened his mouth" people asked, "Could this possibly be the same person who always used to back down at the slightest confrontation? What has happened to him? What has changed him? The fact that *he* is giving this sermon is as remarkable as the sermon itself!"

What was the nature of this change that Peter underwent? Was it that he now had all the answers which he didn't have before? Was it that he no longer cared about his life in this world, because now he understood that heaven and eternal life were all that mattered? On the surface it might seem that this is what it was all about, but not if one looks more deeply. The change, I believe, had to do with Peter's new understanding of *the nature of life itself!*

Like Peter, we all tend to want to live in the safe cocoon where everything is nice and neat, where there are no unsettling surprises, where we have all the answers. We want a Messiah, a Christ, with all the answers as well — we certainly don't want a Christ who will have to suffer and struggle.

Yet the message of Easter in fact does *not* give us all the answers. The message is *not* that we will no longer have to deal with changes and surprises. The message is that now we can truly understand and appreciate the nature of life! Life is *change!* Life is *surprise!* Life is *risk!* In 1 Corinthians 15, St. Paul sums up the Easter message by saying "We shall all be *changed.*" True security, a true sense of rocklike permanance, comes not from hiding in a cocoon, but from learning to appreciate and celebrate life for what it is.

The *surprising paradox* of Easter is that true security and certainty come precisely by facing our shadows, doubts and insecurities. We can be both solid as a rock and Kaleidoscopic as a butterfly at the same time. To celebrate the Resurrection, to celebrate life, is to be no longer afraid of change and *growth!* Easter does not mean that now we can calmly accept death. Easter means that we *defy* death — that *God* defies death — to stop us from changing, from living, from growing! Easter means that we affirm life, *no matter what!*

Some have criticized Christianity for displaying mere wishful thinking in its doctrine of and belief in resurrection. Surveys have shown, however, that *many* people would actually prefer death to be the end! For a variety of reasons I'm sure, it seems that many would prefer not to "meet their Maker," not to face the prospect of eternal life! They would prefer to stay in their cocoons. They would prefer not to change. They would prefer to avoid growing pains. They would prefer, as psychologist Erich Fromm used to say, to "escape from freedom" and from life.

The message of the Resurrection does not call us to a smug security. It calls us to break out of our cocoons. It calls us to embrace life with all its surprises and changes. It calls us to have an open mind about what God can do with our future. The surprising and paradoxical symbol of "the butterfly rock" calls us all to be caught up in the kind of metamorphosis in which Peter was caught up. The message of Easter is that a cocoon is a nice place to be *from!*

2. A Symbol Is A Great Place To Be From

For the next six weeks we are going to be considering some other surprising and paradoxical symbols of Easter. In preparation for this, I would like to share with you the famous description of what a symbol is, which has been left to us by the great theologian, Paul Tillich. Tillich said that we should never use the expression "just" or "merely" or "only" a symbol, because a symbol is more than a *sign* that stands for something else. In contrast to a sign, which can only, merely, *point* to something else, a symbol "*participates* in the reality to which it points!" There is an intrinsic relationship between the symbol and the reality. In a sense, all language about God is and must be symbolic, because by definition, God transcends our understanding. (How many times have we spoken of the peace of God that "passes understanding"?) In other words, our religious symbols are always inadequate — they are negated and affirmed at the same time because they don't say everything but at the same time they say as much as *can* be said! To quote Tillich's own words: "A symbolic expression is one whose proper meaning is negated by that to which it points. And yet it is also affirmed by it, and this affirmation gives the symbolic expression an adequate basis for pointing beyond itself."*

What this perhaps too-high-falutin' language boils down to is that we must always move back and forth between letting symbols

**Systematic Theology Vol. 1*, p. 239.

stand on their own without explanation and yet making the effort to explain what these symbols mean, between celebrating how wonderful symbols are, and yet reminding ourselves how inadequate they are. There has been a lot said in recent years about the need to "demythologize" biblical ideas and stories. That means to explain them "in our own terms." That can be a fine thing to do, and I have done some of it today myself in the first part of this sermon. *But,* as fast as we *de*-mythologize our religious language, we also *re*-mythologize it, because both the *symbol* and the *explaining* of the symbol refer to dimensions of life that are beyond what meets the eye. Whether we use picturesque poetic images or more ordinary prose, what we describe or say remains equally symbolic. I just spoke of a cocoon as a good place to be *from.* What I am saying now is that a *symbol* is a good place to be *from.* Symbols like those which Tillich discusses at length — the Cross, the divine Logos, Justification, "Christus Victor," and the symbols that we will be taking a look at in these next few weeks — all of these Christian symbols are the best starting point we have for coming to grips with the greatest mysteries of life. But to the degree that these symbols participate in dimensions beyond what we experience here and now on this earth, they are only a beginning. They are a good place to be *from,* and they may tell us as much as anything can about where we are going, but they are not "the whole thing." Your name is a great symbol for who you are, but you are more than your name. This understanding of symbols keeps us from taking our limited human perceptions too seriously and keeps us open to future surprises.

The butterfly, and the seed that goes into the earth and dies only to come forth again, are wonderful symbols of Easter. The word Easter itself comes from the name of the Teutonic goddess of Spring, Eastre, and there is a relationship between the dying and rising seed in the spring and the message of Resurrection. Some religions are content merely to point out the convenient analogies between the life-death-rebirth cycles in nature and various aspects of our everyday lives. But for us there is more to Easter than Easter. Easter is the *Resurrection* of *Christ,* and as such it is a *symbol* that points to and participates in dimensions of meaning beyond homely analogy. "Lo, I tell you a mystery!'

Conclusion

Speaking on October 10, 1979, at Harvard Divinity School, Bishop Paulos Gregorios of the Syrian Orthodox Theological Seminary in India, stressed the importance of "trans-rational, trans-conceptual" symbols. "It will be the imaginative creation of adequate symbols and their persistent use in life and worship," he said, "that can protect us against another sweep of . . . cold secular winds . . ."

We are right to explain our faith and apply our faith to the everyday, "secular" world. There is probably no danger of our ever doing too much of that! We can be so heavenly minded that we are no earthly good. But we also need poetic, artistic, theological and other forms of religious symbols to keep our horizons open, to inspire our imaginations as we "consider the heavens."

Next week our Surprising Symbol of Easter will be "Empty Prisons Without Walls." The week after that we will look at "Laughing in Church" as a symbol. And then, our next surprising, paradoxical symbol will be the "Quantum Leap." Until next week. Same time. Same station. By the way, my name means ____________, and the name Jesus means "God Saves." Now there's a tremendous symbol!

(Note: Butterfly pins could be made available to worshipers. Or, a creative project for a church school could be to make "pet rocks" with butterflies painted on them!)

Empty Prisons Without Walls

Introduction

I shouldn't have much trouble keeping you awake today! Since the word *prison* brings to mind such topics as crime, victims' rights, vigilantee justice, and jailed demonstrators, I have little doubt that most of us have strong feelings and opinions on these and related issues.

The most famous line in our text for today brings into particular focus the issue of civil disobedience for the sake of conscience. Having miraculously escaped from prison where they had been placed for disobeying the order not to teach in the name of Jesus, the apostles again find themselves in court. Their famous answer to the charge? "We must obey God rather than men." (Acts 5:29)

A preacher finally confronted one of his parishioners who always slept through his sermons. "You shouldn't take it as an insult," said the sleeper. "My sleeping shows that I trust you completely not to say anything that I might disagree with or be offended by!"

Well, I for one *would* be offended if you never expected anything I say to stimulate, disturb or perhaps even offend you. We live in a complex and often disturbing world, and I think the message of the gospel can and must address these difficult and disturbing problems. The issue of people who demonstrate in the streets or who deliberately break laws in order to do what they believe is right is certainly one of those problems. The standard wisdom regarding such "civil disobedience" today in the United States at least seems to be that all possible orderly means must be used first before one resorts to civil disobedience. Breaking the law, demonstrating in the streets, revolt, must always be seen only as a *last resort* when every other possible means has been used to solve a problem. Writing in the *New York Times Magazine* in 1974, Harvard Law Professor and Watergate prosecutor Archibald Cox stressed that *any* attempt to put one's own sense of morality or justice above the law leads to a crumbling of the moral order from which everyone ultimately suffers. If I think my "cause" is above the law, then the government can think its cause or concern is above the law and then we have the kind of breakdown that leads to Watergate. The equally famous reference in 1 Peter to the fact that Christians should "be subject for the Lord's sake to every human institution" (1 Peter 2:13), including the government, stands beside the apostles' statement about obeying God rather than men. Bishop Eivind Berggrav of Oslo, Norway defied the Nazis and had this to say about "conscientious objection": "Revolt is Christian. But we must turn to it only in cases of necessity . . . not every time something opposes (our) own wishes . . . not just because we are "mutiny-minded." He added, "It is good that revolt or mutiny always involves great outward risk," because we can never underestimate the seriousness of such drastic decisions and actions.

Luther defied Pope and Emperor saying that his conscience was captive to the Word of God. Berggrav goes a step further when he says: "It is inappropriate for Christians to say that if the freedom of the church or of God's Word is not yet directly threatened, we ought not take suffering and strife upon ourselves just for the sake of 'secular matters.' There are no such things as 'secular matters' for a Christian conscience."

I admire the person who risks jail, prison or other great sacrifice for the sake of a deeply-held moral conviction. I understand those who believe that within limits the "demonstration in the street" is just as valid a tool for social change as is the letter to the senator. What I do not admire or respect is the "mutiny-minded" attitude which is simply the childish desire always to have one's own way masquerading under the guise of moral righteousness.

1. Prisons With Walls

There are many reasons why people find themselves in very real prisons with very real walls. The apostles offended those whom they accused of misunderstanding Jesus, and they landed in jail for it.

Martin Luther King spent time in a Birmingham jail. Dietrich Bonhoeffer died in prison at the hands of the Nazis, following his acts of disobedience against the regime.

The majority of people who land in prison do so because they have committed some clear-cut crime. They are in prison because, for a whole host of social and psychological reasons, they have not learned how to cope with life in a positive way. They are a danger to others and to themselves and must be externally restrained by walls, bars, handcuffs.

Then there are those who are political prisoners. They are locked in prisons, mental hospitals or held under "house arrest" because they hold or promote views which appear at least to threaten political or cultural order. Since we are thinking today about symbols and *walls,* we could mix together three *"wall symbols"* here in relation to Poland. Many Polish dissidents are behind prison walls. There is also a tremendous housing shortage in Poland so that we could say that the walls for many more houses need to be built. And yet at the same time the Poles are more busy building church walls — constructing churches — because (we can only guess) the church in Poland has come to symbolize something even more important than the so-called necessities of life like food, clothing and shelter! The church has come to be the ultimate symbol for freedom and life itself. (We might do well to ask ourselves if it truly remains the symbol for that in *our* country!)

2. *Prisons Without Walls*

It was the poet Richard Lovelace who penned the verse: "Stone walls do not a prison make, Nor iron bars a cage." He goes on: "If I have freedom in my love, And in my soul am free, Angels alone that soar above Enjoy such liberty."

Unfortunately, we in many ways make ourselves into prisoners without walls. We, for example, make ourselves prisoners of *the past.* We constantly hark back to "the good old days" and make ourselves unnecessarily miserable by acting as if nothing in the present or future could possibly be worth much of anything. Or, we make ourselves prisoners of *the future,* always looking forward to what we will do "some day" but never really getting around to it. We never do *anything* if we never act in the present moment. Both Christian and some Jewish scholars have pointed out that the practice of expecting the Messiah always only in the future can paralyze us into total inaction in the present. We need to appreciate the sense in which the Savior, the Messiah, *has* come. This is what the high priest and the council in our text had refused to do. Yet, ironically, we can also be prisoners of *the present* by expecting too much from the present.

I often visit with people who are in convalescent hospitals and extremely limited in what they can do. They often seem to regret the fact that most of their few pleasures come from remembering the past or from occasionally anticipating a future visit. I find it very helpful in these situations to remind people that *most* of the pleasures in life for all of us are, after all, symbolic. That is, whatever our age or physical condition, we tend to get most of our pleasure either from remembering the past or from anticipating the future. When we are younger we spend a *great deal* of our time looking forward to what we are *going to do.* When we are older we tend to spend somewhat more time remembering what *has happened before.* But either way, the point is that the present moment itself is often not particularly exciting! In a northern state like Minnesota, one is apt to spend more time watching golf on TV than playing it. Much of our joy in the present moment is provided by symbols — intangible memories and anticipations. Understanding delayed or vicarious gratification is a major part of learning how not to be bored!

Sometimes we become prisoners without walls by behaving as slaves to the *status quo,* to convention and mediocrity. Woody Allen's clever fake documentary about the phenomenal Leonard *Zelig,* told the story of a man who was "the human chameleon." He had the amazing ability to mimic his surroundings and become exactly like whomever he was near. Rich Little, the impersonator, once did a TV movie in which he played the part of an impressionist who had no persona of his own but could only pretend to be other people. One can also be a prisoner without walls in the opposite sense by being a compulsive non-conformist. Always needing to be different can be as much a slavery as always needing to fit in, to be accepted or to be like other people.

3. Empty Prisons

The message of Easter is not only a story of the Empty Tomb. It is also a string of stories about empty prisons. On the quite literal level, as Christians we are concerned about the issues related to crime and punishment. We are concerned to understand the causes of crime and what can be done both to *prevent* people from becoming criminals in the first place, and to *protect* society from the violent and harmful acts of those who have in fact become criminals. We work to support and educate parents so that children will be raised by people who can really get them off to a good start. We face the problems of poverty and unemployment and depression, realizing that these are the most common breeding-grounds of crime. We want to keep prisons empty by struggling to overcome the evils in society!

Our Christian faith and commitment also motivate us to understand and work against political and economic oppression. Vigilant opponents of all forms of totalitarianism, we resist the urge to lock up or ostracize everyone who strongly criticizes our culture, our governnment, our "way of life." It can be very difficult to resist the temptation to want to lock in a prison or mental hospital, or to ostracize, everyone who questions some basic values or traditions of our society, but if we keep reminding ourselves of the ways in which that is done in totalitarian countries perhaps we can avoid this trap.

Prisons are both the reality and the symbol of our *failures.* Remember Ebeneezer Scrooge's disturbing attitude: "Are there no workhouses? Are there no prisons?" Surely in the Kingdom of God there will be no more prisons and God will "bless us, every one."

4. Empty Prisons Without Walls

The emptying of the prisons *which have no walls,* however, is the *ultimate* effect of Easter. To be freed from the prison of the past, the future, the present, the *status quo,* the mutiny-mentality — that is true freedom and life. To be released by Christ's forgiveness from the prisons of guilt, fear, anger, negative fixations and low self-esteem — this is the most subtle, the most personal, and finally the most significant impact of the Easter message. In the last analysis it is always our *attitudes* that make us prisoners. Paradoxically, it is the prisons without walls that are the most confining, that are the most difficult to empty. It is our failures in love that create prisons far more restrictive than stone walls.

As happened with the Apostles, our Christian faith can get us in trouble, but it also frees us from all trouble! Our faith can make us *go* to jails, *visit* jails (remember that Jesus said we visit him when we visit prisoners), and work *to eliminate the need* for jails. (Remember that the first thing Jesus did after his death according to 1 Peter 3:19 was to "preach to the spirits in prison," an image which has meaning on a number of levels.) As with the Apostles, when the God of love is by our side, we can walk through the doors and walls of all prisons as if they weren't even there. We can break down "the dividing wall of hostility . . . so making peace." (Ephesians 2:14-15)

Conclusion

A number of poets have done variations on the theme, "Stone walls do not a prison make." The writer of one very old Christian hymn could be included in this group. Some of the stanzas began with the line "Faith of our Fathers," and some of the stanzas began with the line "Faith of our Mothers," so I will combine the two and quote perhaps the hymn's most memorable line this way: "Our ancestors chained in prisons dark, were still in heart and conscience free!" They were truly free in that they were ultimately free from both kinds of prisons, the prisons *with* walls and the prisons *without* walls.

Laughing In Church

Introduction

Long before the Dean Martin Celebrity Roasts came on the scene, I had been seeing preachers "roasted" at church banquets. The idea of honoring someone by kidding or insulting the person is nothing new. At a recent convention a United Methodist bishop (I'll call him Bishop Anderson) was roasted with this story: A recent Methodist arrival in heaven was being shown around by St. Peter. A couple minutes into the tour he saw an old friend of his. But it was a disturbing sight. Attached to his friends leg by a large chain was the most hideous blob of sticky protoplasm he had ever seen. *"What is that?"* he asked St. Peter, scarcely able to control his horror. "Oh," said St. Peter. "Well, you see your friend was far from perfect in his life on earth and this is his punisnment." A little further on the man saw another friend with an even more hideous blob attached to his leg. "I guess Leo did quite a few bad things in his life too, eh?" "I'm afraid so," St. Peter responded. Going on the man suddenly recognized Bishop Anderson, who also had a chain attached to his leg. But at the other end of the chain was Dolly Parton! "My goodness!" exclaimed the tourist. "Bishop Andeison must have been a very good fellow while he was on earth to receive Dolly Parton as his reward!" "Oh, no, no," said St. Peter, "you don't understand. It's the other way around. Dolly Parton was very, very bad!"

1. Grace In Church

A great many jokes are based on the principle of the surprise twist. All of a sudden, everything is turned totally upside down. Our perspective is reversed. This sudden "conversion" is exactly what happens to Saul of Tarsus in our text for today. You may never have seen anything particularly funny in this account of the conversion of St. Paul, but there is a certain humor in the image of the rabid persecutor "breathing threats and murder against the disciples of the Lord" suddenly being transformed into the most ardent and eloquent spokesman for Jesus in the history of the world. The changed life of St. Paul, like the changed life of St. Peter, is another of the Surprising Symbols of Easter!

And the central message of St. Paul's preaching and writing was another surprise twist! "By grace are you saved, through faith!" Jesus *lived* grace by associating with and accepting sinners. Paul developed that theme of grace in theological terms. Grace turns our usual, achievement-oriented way of thinking upside down. Grace converts us from being people who take ourselves too seriously into people who trust God to take care of the ultimately serious things. We come to church to hear about the grace of God, and what we learn is how to combine a sense of urgency and seriousness about ourselves, the world and our destiny, with a sense of humor and relaxation about our efforts to improve or heal ourselves and the world.

To live under grace, to be a Christian, to refrain from "breathing threats" and otherwise taking ourselves too seriously, is to have a *sense of humor!* It is true that the word "laugh" itself usually appears in the Bible in reference to scorn laughing *at* the foolishness of those who oppose God. But on the first level today, we want to talk not about laughing, but about "sense of humor" as referring to our fundamental attitude toward life. Jesus is making a comment on humor in this sense when he says: "do not be anxious about your life . . ." (Matthew 6:25) Alan Watts, a leading English/American exponent of Zen Buddhism, liked to emphasize that nature is more *playful* than purposeful. We spoil music for example, he said, if we analyze it too much, if we play it only to get to the end or to improve our performance — if we never simply play, listen and enjoy. Luther said that next to theology, music was the greatest, but I think it might be more profoundly true to say that *playing, music, theology, grace* are all one and the same thing!

The relationship between the theology of grace and the element of humor has been brought out in many different ways. There is Dante's *Divine Comedy*. In 1964 D. Elton Trueblood published *The*

Humor of Christ, in which he showed how Jesus used humor in his parables and in his encounters with critics. Harvey Cox celebrated humor, fantasy and festivity in his book *The Feast of Fools.* Robert Short has become famous as the theologian who writes books and gives lectures on the theology in the *Peanuts* cartoon strip. The play and film *Godspell* used clown imagery to tell "the greatest story ever told." The president of the Presbyterian seminary in San Anselmo, California, Arnold Come, summed up his extensive encounters with the great Karl Barth by saying that "God's man must be joyful above all." The very last words of his book discussing Barth's massive *Dogmatics* describe Barth as a man "of rare good humor." A surprise! One could have expected such a "serious theologian" to be stuffy and dull.

Now, telling jokes and being humorous can be a great way to make friends. But it can also be one of the easiest ways to offend people. If Bishop Anderson (in the joke just told) was extremely self-conscious about his lack of good looks, he might have laughed on the surface but cried underneath when he was "honored" with this insult humor. There is almost always a grain of truth in humor that is critical, and this truth can hurt. The drunk can be funny, pathetic and tragic all at the same time. When the Gospel of John says that "grace and truth" came by Jesus Christ, it means in part that grace helps us to bear the truth — not to be afraid of even painful truths — and it means that our knowledge of the truth *can* make us whole and free again.

Last Christmas I sent some friends a card that showed Mary, Joseph and the babe in the manger under the star, with Joseph saying to Mary: "Quit complaining! What did you expect with a one-star hotel?" Inside the card I wrote: "To be 'full of grace,' is to have a sense of humor." Now I suspect some people might be offended by this kind of "religious" humor. But I stand by the card and would insist that far from being sacreligious it is in fact a wonderful expression of the gospel of grace in Christ that we learn about in church. The Christmas message is "good tidings of great *joy!*"

2. *Humor in Church*

In order to see the place of humor in the church, in religion, and in the Bible, we must learn to see and appreciate humor in various forms and on different levels. The word "laugh" does not appear often in the Bible, but words like "joy" and "rejoice," and expressions like "making merry" and "celebrating a feast" appear many, many times. The parable of the servant who was forgiven a two-million dollar debt only to imprison the fellow who owed him a quarter, was a funny joke told to drive home a point about the importance of forgiveness. But most of the humor in the Scriptures takes more subtle forms.

There is irony, wit, satire, sarcasm, the pun, the enigma, absurdity, and (as Louie Crew says in an article entitled *Did Jesus Laugh?),* "the crafty rhetorical gymnastics of the jive artist." In this wonderful article, Crew describes Jesus, the Lord who turned St. Paul's life upside down, as "the boisterous rule-breaker" who used subtly funny verbal games to keep his legalistic oppressors and critics off guard. "Give to Caesar the things that are Caesar's and unto God the things that are God's" is more riddle than answer! Crew also notes Jesus' relish for farce and sarcasm, as in his picture of the person with a log in his own eye trying to remove the speck in his brother's eye. Then there is humorous exaggeration (hyperbole) in the image of his detractors as moralists who "strain out gnats yet swallow camels!" Crew concludes that the one who wittily dubbed his followers "fishers of men" clearly must have laughed, celebrated and rejoiced a great deal.

Some years ago in a newspaper column, the then Episcopal Bishop of Michigan, Richard Emrich, wrote in praise of "those who cheer us up" with humor. "But," he went on to say, "we do not laugh if a matter is too serious," if it is an "ultimate matter." "I do not want laughter at the altar . . . in life's deepest moments. If it occurs in these places, then it is cheap, cynical and even blasphemous." Now we're getting serious about this business of humor!

I believe that Bishop Emrich's understanding of humor is too limited. Far from being out of place in regard to serious, ultimate matters, I would say that *it is our very ability to maintain a profound sense of humor no matter how bad or serious things get for us, that is the ultimate secret of coping with life!* Many poets, philosophers and writers of various kinds have suggested that we have much to gain from looking at the world as a huge "cosmic joke" which God is playing on us. To some this means that the creation of the world is more God's *play* than God's *work*. The point then is that if we can maintain a lighter attitude, which is content "to win a few and lose a few," we will be able to roll with the punches and survive much better. I think there is something right about this approach, in the sense that it is saying that we should not take ourselves too seriously on *any* level.

But it is the *cynicism* of this "cosmic joke" idea that intrigues me most. In his book *The Comic Vision and the Christian Faith,* Conrad Hyers says that "faith without laughter leads to dogmatism and self-righteousness" and that "laughter without faith leads to cynicism." The ultimate point of the "cosmic joke" idea is that *God understands our cynicism!* Far from denying and avoiding all traces of cynicism, the Christian faith is wonderful precisely because it allows us to face and deal with even our most profound cynicism and despair! There is an entire book of cynicism in the Bible. *Ecclesiastes,* in the Old Testament, with its "Vanity of vanities, all is vanity" teaches us not to deny our cynicism.

If we only use humor to "laugh off" our small vexations we have failed totally to understand "sense of humor" as an expression of God's grace! Just using a little humor to "lighten your day" is like the shallow gospel which has nothing to offer but naive optimism and "positive thinking." Steve Allen says that "comedy is tragedy plus time." Having a truly profound sense of humor means that I can face all the tragic ironies of life, all the confusing paradoxes of life, the absurdities of life, all the reasons to be cynical — *and still not lose faith!* Our challenge is *not* to avoid cynical laughter, but to be able to *transform* cynical laughter into *insight* that overcomes our cynicism *as we laugh!* This is true conversion. This is truly turning things and the world upside down in the wonderful way that God wants us to turn it upside down.

Saul of Tarsus had come to the point of utter cynicism in his efforts to deal with the followers of Jesus. He who thought he knew everything suddenly realized he was blind. In becoming Paul the apostle, he converted cynical derision into faith. He had laughed *at* the Christians. Now he could relax and laugh *with* them.

It's time to say something nice about a bishop. Lowell Erdahl, a Lutheran Bishop in Minnesota, has written an insightful pamphlet called *Paradoxes of Living.* The paradoxes and inconsistencies in life give us many reasons to be cynical. But as faith transforms cynicism into a positive ironic sense of humor, so faith also transforms frustrating contradictions into meaningful paradoxes and holy inconsistencies. Listen to some of the paradoxes Erdahl discusses: (1) The most happiness comes to those who realize they will not always be happy. (2) Confessing our weakness is an evidence and source of strength. (3) To enjoy being together we need to be alone. (4) We lengthen our days by remembering the shortness of our years. (5) Victory often comes through surrender. Part of what it takes to appreciate these kinds of paradoxes and incorporate them in our lives is a profound sense of humor. Far from saying that humor is out of place in church, I think we have to say that it is in church where humor receives its most profound validation.

3. Laughing In Church

But the question still remains: can — or should — we actually *laugh* in church? You know, that question is a little like asking if we should "really believe" the message of the gospel or just pretend to believe. Soren Kirkegaard created a memorable satire of the geese who went every Sunday to hear lectures on flying and then went home to eat a huge dinner. They loved the speeches and they loved to eat, but they *never* got around to actually flying! I've heard the same idea applied to people who read books about swimming but never actually go in the water.

We can't always just talk about joy and laughing! Perhaps one of these days we should have a joke-fest during the sermon time in the same way that we sometimes have a hymn-sing! (Tell me what you think of the idea.) We could share jokes and/or humorous anecdotes that have given us insight. The laughter would be a liturgical act. We could even do some liturgical applause at the end of such a sermon. It might be a surprise. But it would *not* be out of place. Conrad Hyers claims that laughter and a comic perspective are uniquely human attributes. I think he's right and I think we need to celebrate this attribute — literally! Speaking of comic perspective, try this on for size: We need *imagination* to help us deal with what we are *not* and a *sense of humor* to help us deal with what we *are.*

A character in the documentary film, *Word Is Out,* describes our laughter as akin to the barking of a dog. There may be something instinctual about it. Another explanation of what laughter itself is (one which means more to me) suggests that the impulse to laugh is the same as the impulse to cry. When a parent teasingly throws a child up in the air the first few times, the child cries. But then the infant quickly learns that the parent is just joking. So now instead of crying the infant giggles or laughs when his original impulse had been to cry. According to this theory of laughter, the infant converts the impulse to cry into the impulse to laugh when she knows she's safe.

To give an example from the "other end" of life, we can laugh at cemetery jokes whenever we are not numb in the midst of grief because, although there is a frightening aspect to death, we are not immediately threatened by death. We laugh because we know that for the time being at least we are safe from the thing that frightens us. This is why and how humor both hurts and heals. It touches often on our sore points while at the same time, if we are lucky, it helps us come to terms with our weaknesses and fears and hurts.

This is why there are inevitably arguments about when and where humor is appropriate. Sometimes it both helps and hurts to laugh. From this observation about the relation of crying and laughing, I think it follows that to banish laughter from church is like banishing children from the worship service. When Jesus told the little children to come to him I'm sure he knew there would be a lot of laughing and crying.

Now above all, of course, in this series of sermons on *The Surprising Symbols of Easter* I am using the phrase "Laughing In Church" as a *symbol,* a symbol for the joyful life that God gives us as a gift of grace. To have a real sense of humor does not mean that we are always laughing. It *does* mean that we need never lose our *ability* to laugh. To have a profound sense of humor is to know that the "bottom line" for the Christian is not *grim* but *grace*. The symbol of "Laughing In Church" *is* a criticism of all those humorless preachers and groups that remain painfully serious even when they talk about joy, if they talk about it at all. Louie Crew even describes the Resurrection as "a laughter at death itself."

"Oh death, where is thy sting?" "Women, why are you weeping?" Surely the Easter season especially is a time for laughing — *at* death and *with* life!

Conclusion

We have read today the story of the conversion of St. Paul, from grim, rigid legalist to apostle of grace. And we have seen that to live in the light of God's grace is to have a sense of humor about *everything*. We may not always need to laugh literally to express or reflect this good humor, but on the other hand we need not be overly hesitant to laugh either. In the book of *Psalms* we read of how people sang and *danced* and made music before the Lord. We often hear the admonition "Smile, God loves you." If dancing, singing and smiling are appropriate in church, then so is laughing!

The other day I was forcefully reminded of *God's* sense of humor. I said to God, "Is it true that with you one minute is like a thousand years?" And God said "Yes." So I asked, "Would it also be true then that to you a single dollar would be like a million dollars?" "Yes, that's right." "Well then," I said to God, "could I please have a dollar?" And God said, "Wait a minute!"

Quantum Leap

Introduction

The evidence is everywhere: we have made a *quantum leap* into "the age of the computer." In schools, hospitals, businesses, publishers, even local and national church offices, everything is "computerized," digitalized, programmed. You may be fascinated by computer technology or you may hate this computer craze. But none of us can escape a concern with the impact this "revolution" is having on our lives. (The other day I had to wait about three minutes for the clerk at Kentucky Fried Chicken to figure out how to register my discount coupon in her push-button cash register.)

In a way, not all that much has changed. A phone call is still a phone call even if the phone itself is more elaborate. Typing is still typing even if a word processor makes it more efficient. It could be argued that *what* we do has not been changed at all, only the *way* we do it. But in some ways, everything has changed. Your entire business or personal life may be radically altered by the phone call your answering machine caught — a call that you would have missed if you didn't have the recorder.

Computers can also have a profound influence on our lives in the way they affect our attitudes. Computers can free us from much drudgery and give us more time for personal, *human* things. They can free us to be human. But they can also have the opposite effect. If you work all day with efficient computers and come home at night to a family of human beings who aren't always so efficient, logical or "programmable," you might become very angry with these people precisely for being "so human." The computer can make *me* into a computer, another cog in the machinery of modern life, *less* human instead of *more* human. This tension between the computer as a *humanizing* or as a *dehumanizing* influence is one of the growing conflicts in our life that requires more and more of our conscious attention.

1. The Thin Line Between a Small Change and a Huge Change

Computer technology is based on modern electronics and modern physics, and at the heart of modern physics is the "theory of quantum mechanics." *Quantum theory* refers to our understanding of the way in which sub-atomic particles, electrons in particular, make sudden, tiny, unpredictable "jumps." One of the smartest scholars in the world, Persi Diaconis at Stanford University, is writing a book called *Coincidences* in which he is delving into such things as the relationship between quantum mechanics and so-called psychic phenomenon. This ability of sub-atomic particles to pop up anywhere, any time, by taking a quantum leap between unconnected levels of energy, means that effects do not always have causes, that there is a principle of freedom at work in the universe *and in the human mind!* Some thinkers suggest that we should view God as directing these sudden bursts, changes, surprises. In this framework, God's raising of Jesus *could* be compared to those instances where a brilliant idea suddenly hits you like "a bolt out of the blue." A surprising, unpredictable new possibility materializes when a creative quantum leap is made.

I am no expert on quantum physics, so now it is time to focus on the main reason why I have chosen the phrase "Quantum Leap" as one of the Surprising Symbols of Easter. The quantum leap not only brings surprise results; the quantum leap is also a surprise because it is a paradox! Most people tend to use the expression "quantum leap" to signify a huge change, a tremendous stride forward. The fact is that "quantum" actually refers to a *tiny* change, the very tiniest movement possible in the tiniest particle of matter. The paradox is that both of these definitions of the "quantum leap" are correct. The quantum leap is *the small change* that can result in a *huge* change! It is the study of the smallest particles of matter that has led us into "the atomic age" with its almost unbelievable possibilities and its haunting terrors. Our world has been turned upside down by what we have learned through the microscope.

In many ways, the good news of the gospel that Paul and the

apostles of Jesus were preaching was not all that different from what Israel, the people of God, had always known and believed. After all, in our text, the law, the prophets, the synagogue, are all affirmed, and, reading on, we discover that many were prepared to hear and understand and appreciate the insights that Paul shares in this message. The theme of God's loving kindness and mercy — God's grace — was nothing new to "the family of Abraham." The small change suggested by the followers of Jesus was that now this theme of God's grace was to "take center stage" in a way that it hadn't before. They were preaching about a tiny change that would make a huge difference, a Quantum Leap.

Many years after the publication of his novel on which the play and film *Cabaret* is based, Christopher Isherwood wrote a memoir in which he gives a look behind the scenes of his original stories. He was not saying that the novel had been all wrong. He was simply enlarging the portrait, shifting the focus. In a similar way, Paul in his sermon here is not saying that the faith of Abraham and Moses was all wrong. He simply was saying that people had failed to *recognize* Jesus and his message for what it was. The word "recognize" means to "look again," to take a new or second look. The message of Jesus was that people needed to climb out of their rut and take a new look at what their tradition was leading toward.

2. *Quantum Leap Out Of A Rut*

Apparently, moral and spiritual blindness are a chronic problem for God's people. Jesus had challenged Israel to jump out of her rut: Go beyond "an eye for an eye." Love your enemies. When the occasion calls for it, be ready to do the unexpected thing and "turn the other cheek." Take another look at what Law and Covenant are all about. Take another look at what the idea of "Messiah" means. Maybe Messiah is more like "the Suffering Servant" of Isaiah than like King David. Or could it be that Messiah is like *both* images? Such a complex and paradoxical notion would be hard to comprehend, to "see."

There is a thin line between a genius and a moron. (The word "sophomore" comes from the Greek *sophos,* meaning "wise" and *moros* which means "fool." A sophomore is halfway between stupid and smart.) Almost every founder of a great world religion has been judged crazy at some point. In the Gospel of Mark we read that at times even Jesus' friends and family thought he was "beside himself," that is, off his rocker, and, of course, many of the sons of Abraham were sure that Yeshua (as they would have called Jesus) was indeed crazy.

Those of us who have come to know the grace and love of God through Jesus know that he was "crazy like a fox." We clearly see him on the "genius" side of that thin line between wise one and fool. We know that, spiritually speaking, Jesus made a quantum leap and that by bringing God's grace to center stage in a unique way, Jesus has made a small change in our perspective, one that radically alters our attitude. We know that God still wants us to do his will, to do good works, to do our best, but that *the attitude* in which we do what we do is never any longer one of *earning* God's favor, but of *responding* to God's unmerited favor. We are not discouraged by God's high moral demands because we know that God does not intend them to discourage us! We know that God wants us to learn the "trick" of combining great effort with an ability to relax, the "trick" of combining a sense of urgency with a sense of humor.

It wasn't only the people in Jesus' day who resisted climbing out of their ruts. How open are *we* to new insights?

Jesus never asked or expected his fellow Jews totally to give up their traditional beliefs. His message was only that they needed to take a new look, get a new slant on what their tradition was all about! The "quantum leap" that his message called for was not a huge change, but it *seemed like* a tremendous change to those who opposed him. Changing the main focus from *law* to *grace* seemed like a radical change, and it *was,* but only in the sense that a quantum leap is at the same time *both* a small *and* a great change! Our text for today is about the failure to be open to new insights regarding things that are of central importance to us. It can be rather easy to make changes regarding peripheral matters. But God also calls us to *re*-view even fundamental ideas that we thought were settled.

Let's ask ourselves, for example, how we might need to climb out of *our* familiar rut in relation to the understanding of our *mission* as Christians. Is it our calling to "make everyone Christian," to hammer away at the theme that everyone who does not "accept Christ" is lost and condemned? *Or,* does believing in Jesus mean to believe that salvation is God's business? Does believing in Jesus mean to believe that it is *not our job* to judge who is or can be saved? If we understand the gospel of grace to mean that the only way to be saved is *by God,* then it becomes clear that *we cannot put limits on who God can save!* The name "Jesus," which we celebrate and worship, means "God saves!" If we view our mission as a matter of witnessing to the *meaning* of this "name that is above every name," then I think we will be making an important and needed quantum leap in our approach to Christian witnessing!

3. A Tiny Distinction Can Make A Big Difference

There is often a thin line between witnessing and bigotry! A tiny distinction between one approaach to "evangelism" and another can make a big difference. We can offer Christ as "the answer" in such a way that we come across as holier-than-thou know-it alls. Or we can witness to Christ in an open spirit of *dialogue.* Think of the times you have been confronted by "witnesses" who are obviously hoping to *manipulate* you into buying their particular version of religion. Do you then feel as though you are truly being treated as a person? Or, instead, as an object to be "collected"?

The time has come to realize that "hard-sell" evangelism is both bad theology and bad method. It is bad theology because it is not our calling to "save the world." It is bad method because most people in our world are sick and tired of those who tell them they are lost if you don't agree with them. In short, most people do not find bigotry attractive.

If anyone is saved, God does it. Saving the world is ultimately God's business. We can invite people to church. We can share our faith with others or discuss theology and religion just as we would discuss other subjects. We can love. We can share. We can work for justice. But *we* cannot "save" anyone! It is a contradiction in terms to make the message of Jesus into any form of bigotry. Christians do not have all the answers. We *do* have good reasons to enter into dialogue with people about the grace of God. People do not resent open dialogue. People do not resent graciousness that has no strings attached. Such graciousness is a surprise. Such graciousness is our message and our medium.

Conclusion

Niels Bohr, the great Danish physicist who pioneered with quantum physics and helped lay the groundwork for the atomic age, is also remembered for his quip: "Some things are so serious you can only joke about them." Sharing our experience of the grace of God is a serious matter. Yet at the same time this grace is the most profound basis for a sense of humor. God's grace makes it possible for us to be the kind of adults who never forget what it means to be like children (sons and daughters of God) who don't take themselves too seriously. God's grace makes it possible for us to make quantum leaps back and forth between opposites like seriousness and humor, struggle and relaxation, trusting ourselves and trusting God — recognizing that the distinction between such opposites is both tiny and tremendous. Both sides belong, but it makes all the difference that a "gracious humor" which relaxes and trusts God is the bottom line for us.

Niels Bohr did not consider himself to be a particularly religious man. He once joked about Albert Einstein, who often referred to God in his writing and lectures, with the line: "Albert should quit telling God what to do." Einstein himself liked to say: "Imagination is more important than intelligence." What a gracious, humble sense of humor both of those great scientists had! May we reflect that same gracious humor in our lives. That's what the quantum leap between depending on ourselves and depending on God is all about.

Some Illusions [Symbols] Are Better Than Others

Introduction

Sigmund Freud said that God is an illusion. We take the idea of a loving father, he said, project it upon the universe, and call it God. Today's text from Acts bears witness to this process of creating gods by means of personification and projection. (A humorous way of criticizing our tendency to create God or gods in *our* image goes like this: "God created mankind in his image, and mankind returned the compliment!")

I'm afraid we have to confess that all of us — not just the people in Lystra — have a well-demonstrated ability to picture God the way we would like God to be. One glaring example of this is the tendency to insist that God is *male,* in spite of the numerous biblical indications that God is beyond gender distinctions. The Greeks made no bones about that fact that their gods were anthropomorphic. Their gods were larger than life and they were immortal, but in every other respect they were "very human." The people of Lystra assumed Paul was a representative of the god Hermes because Hermes was identified in their minds with science, invention, cunning, trickery, luck *and eloquence.* In the old, classic movie, *The African Queen,* the Katharine Hepburn character says to the Humphrey Bogart character: "Nature is what we were put in this world to rise above!" In their glorification of the natural world and of human nature, the Greeks demonstrated their failure to see the element of truth in Katharine Hepburn's line. If the concept of God does not in some way point beyond nature, then "God" is indeed an illusion, a figment of mankind's overactive imagination. A truly *Living God* is going to push us to and beyond the limits of our understanding. The idea of such a Living God moves beyond being a mere illusion, to being a *Symbol.*

Surprisingly, Freud admitted that *his own* ideas were *also* illusions! He recognized that his notions, like the "Oedipus Complex," were what psychologists call artificial *constructs.* They are, in other words, a symbolic, shorthand way of describing certain complex patterns of human behavior that cannot actually be simplified. As an attempt to simplify that which cannot be simplified (since every person is complex and unique), Freud admitted that his own ideas were illusions. They were inadequate, deceptive and "unreal" in the sense that they were abstract and over-simplified. Freud thought that both God *and* his (Freud's) ideas were illusions. But then he added: "My illusions are *better than* the religious illusions!"

What Freud meant by this statement was that, in our day, the so-called social sciences — psychology and sociology — are more effective than theology in handling the things that religion has traditionally dealt with: our human needs for security, reassurance, self-understanding, values, coping with problems, and the like. But today, every major seminary teaches future ministers courses on psychology and pastoral care. For many of us it is clear that theology and psychology can work hand in hand.

The issue is not really a matter of whose illusions are better, but rather what is the relationship between an *illusion* and a *symbol.* Both terms can be defined in opposite ways. We can speak of "mere" illusions or "mere" symbols, implying that both are unreal. Or we can stress with theologian Paul Tillich that, while both illusions and symbols are *inadequate* and partial reflections of the truth, they do *participate* in the greater or deeper reality to which they point! From this latter point of view, illusions and symbols are not *purely* deceptive and unreal; they are, rather, "deceptively simple" and "partial pictures" of reality!

Once we have understood this sense in which illusions and symbols can *both* be positive things, we can begin to discuss the ways in which some symbols/illusions may be better than others — both in psychology and in theology.

One of the greatest false symbols or *idols* of our culture today, is *success.* Much television evangelism, falls into the trap of equating faith in God with all kinds of success. The Bible and its advice becomes something like a religious version of *How To Win Friends and Influence People.* A major college football coach (who will remain unnamed) has been known to give "spiritual pep-talks" on the lecture circuit. The gospel according to this "preacher" is: Do what is right. Do your best. Treat others as you would like to be treated — and you'll be amazed at how successful you will be in life! The ordained preachers who constantly trot out spiritual, business or other kinds of "athletes" are also creating this "Success Image," this "Success Symbol" of God, and even though they may try to "spiritualize" the idea of success, the fact is that they have made success itself into their central symbol! Instead of dethroning the great God SUCCESS, most such preaching simply reverses the order — don't look for material success first and spiritual success last; look for spiritual success first and then you will be surprised at how successful you will be in material ways.

What's wrong with success? I hear you saying. Nothing is wrong with success, but that doesn't mean that success is God, that success is even an *adequate* symbol for what faith is all about. There is nothing wrong with celebrating success, but success has its costs and in some ways we often need to be saved even from our success! By its very nature, our success may put us in the position of deliberately or inadvertantly stepping on other people's toes. *Faith* may not have so much to do with achieving success as with being faithful to a concern for love and justice as we try to do what is best *for us. Faithfulness* to God's will, that we "love one another," is a much better symbol than *success!*

The popular composer Irving Berlin once said that "the toughest thing about success is that you've got to keep on *being* a success." Success, far from being the gospel, may become a burden to which the gospel is the answer. Early during 1985 there were quite a few lengthy television programs preaching the gospel of success through real estate speculation. The message was hammered home that all you need is the desire to succeed, hard work, and information and "you can be a millionaire!" One testamonial came from a man who said he now had his business on his mind virtually twenty-four hours a day but that he was nevertheless happier than he was when working a simple eight-hour day. In other words, the "business-success" promoters try to get you committed to an aggressive style of life wherein you become a certain type of person. How many such people realize that they may be selling their soul to a way of life?

It's easy to imagine people getting in over their heads and needing to be saved from their "success."

Paul and Barnabas were successful in helping a lame man to walk, but in one sense they immediately regretted this success. The people of Lystra wanted to worship them, whereas their goal had been to get the people to worship the living God. Ironically, success was getting in the way of the gospel.

In the case of the lame man himself, it was his *faith* that impressed Paul. Throughout the New Testament, the individual's faith is consistently portrayed as being more important than the miracle. Successful signs and miracles are secondary to faith. In this instance, Paul and Barnabas might have wanted to undo the miracle, but I am certain that they would *not* have wanted to undo the faith that they had seen in the lame man. The miracle had become an illusion in the sense that it was deceptive and misleading. The real thing, the man's faith, was missed by the people of Lystra who then proceeded to compound their mistake by not listening to Barnabas and Pauls' explanation of what real faith is all about.

Doug Henning prefers to be described as an illusionist rather than as a magician. His "philosophy of magic" is that the purpose of magic is to create a sense of wonder. The trick that produces the amazement or wonder may simply be an illusion, a total "fake-out." But however it is produced, the *sense of wonder* itself is real! He wants his audiences to enjoy the illusions. But, more important, he wants to help people develop their sense of wonder toward all the real "magic" in the world, all the deeper miracles such as beauty, love and faith. The former U.N. Secretary General Dag Hammarskjold was thinking along similar lines when he wrote: "God does not die on the day when we cease to believe in a personal deity, but *we* die on the day when our lives cease to be illuminated by the steady radiance, renewed daily, of *a wonder,* the source of which is beyond all reason."

Conclusion

Success and failure are relative things. The harlot or hustler mentality may make you a success, but if all your human relationships are translated into business exchanges your life will be shallow and empty. In both *Equus* and *Amadeus,* playwrite Peter Shaffer is commenting on this relativity of success and failure in life. The psychiatrist in *Equus* knows he can "cure" the boy, but he wonders if this crazy, passionate boy isn't actually better off than he, the drab, well-adjusted pillar of society. In *Amadeus* we see Salieri, the "success," and Mozart, the "failure." But who was the truly successful one? Which one was really favored by God? And what a wonderful multiplication of ironies that the actor who played Salieri in the film won the Academy Award, not the one who played Mozart! The important thing obviously is not to choose which of the characters in *Equus* or *Amadeus* was "successful." "Success or failure" is simply not an adequate symbol or category for judging a person's worth or importance. The sardonic joke that describes Jesus as "a flop at 33" is another excellent reminder of how insignificant success or failure is from a divine perspective. Faith and forgiveness are much more important criteria and symbols than success. Seen on a more profound level, Henry Ford was talking about faith and forgiveness when he said, "Failure is only thc opportunity to begin again, more intelligently." To speak of God's faithfulness and forgiveness is to realize that it is what God can accomplish through us that counts; to realize that there is always another chance, that there is always hope, that whether we succeed or fail, God is with us and God's presence is all we really need. In our most intimate personal relationships it is much more important that we be loved and trusted than that we be "successful." Both psychologically and theologically speaking, faithfulness and love are much better symbols than success!

Concrete Abstractions

Introduction

Do you like modern, abstract art? There's no question about it: abstract art can be difficult to appreciate or understand. One key to understanding this kind of artistic representation is to remember that the word "abstract" means to *choose from,* to *draw* or *separate from.* The abstract artist *chooses* a particular aspect of his or her subject matter and in so doing alters our usual perception, changes the proportions so as to highlight specific things. The problem, therefore, with much abstract art is not that it is too vague, too general, too "abstract." The problem is that it is too specific, too selective, too "concrete." A photographer can take an extremely close-up picture of your face and you might not be able to recognize who it is precisely because it is such a close shot. One of the jobs of the artist is to help us see things from new or different angles so that we might understand them better. Actually this is what any thinker or scientist does.

1. "To abstract" is to choose or epitomize what is important, significant, enduring

I have a small quarrel with those who chose, who "abstracted", the portions of Acts chapter 15 that we are to read for our text today. It seems to me that they left out the most salient verse, verse eleven, which reads: "We believe that we shall be saved through the grace of the Lord Jesus, just as they will." One of the most persistent issues in the entire New Testament has to do with whether the gospel is for Jews only and whether converts are expected to obey all the traditional Jewish laws. The answers to these questions became more and more clear. We *cannot* choose to share the good news only with a select few, but we *can* choose, we can decide which laws remain relevant for us in our specific situations. The gist of Acts 15 is that when God's grace in the Lord Jesus takes center stage, we are freed to make the ethical decisions that fit our own situation.

In this early period of transition, the church chose remarkably few general rules: "abstain from what has been sacrificed to idols and from blood and from what is strangled and from unchastity." What a shock it must have been that circumcision was no longer to be *required!* What a remarkable degree of "freedom in Christ" the early church preached! What myriad choices the simple law of love and empathy places before us! The very fact that "the apostles and the elders, with the whole church" met together and discussed and decided these questions of law and ethics is perhaps more important than the specific conclusions to which they came. As the world has changed, the issue of "meat sacrificed to idols" has become much less significant. The important thing is that in our story for today we see the early church setting the pattern for what George Forell has called *Ethics of Decision* (Muhlenberg Press, 1955). To live in, with and under the grace of the Lord Jesus involves learning to separate out the "weightier matters of the law," to make choices in accordance with the spirit, not just the letter of the law; to engage in the process of discussion and dialogue for the purpose of making informed ethical choices and value judgments. To live in the grace of the Lord Jesus is to be free to abstract — to choose — what is important, significant, enduring and good out of all that which surrounds us. We're likely to disagree with one another once in a while, just as I disagree with those abstractors who left verse eleven out of our text; but as long as the grace and love of God guides us we can't go too far wrong. We can debate and discuss what chastity means and in what sense it remains an important issue in our day, without insisting that everyone come to exactly the same conclusions.

2. *"Abstract" and "Concrete" Are Opposites*

Now while it is true that the basic meaning of "abstract" is to choose or separate something out from the whole and that, therefore, an abstraction can be extremely concrete, the word does also refer to something that is theoretical as *opposed* to concrete. In art, this can mean that the artist will use geometric figures or diagrams to picture aspects of our human experience that we usually do not think of in such patterned, theoretical, abstract, *symbolic* ways. Drawing a triangle to represent the Trinity, for example, does not mean that God is a triangle. This abstract symbol focuses on only one aspect of what our language about God means.

You are probably already tired of this talk about concrete and abstract. Such a discussion is itself too abstract. Perhaps most of you feel that you would rather simply pray to God in the concrete than analyze God in the abstract. Most of our conversations with our friends are about specific feelings and events. I want a friend who will listen and empathize as I tell about my frustration with a child who won't do her homework. I don't want an abstract discussion on the various approaches to child-rearing. We live in the present moment, and it is good to get down to cases. How terrible it would be to watch all kinds of TV programs about good cooking, but never bother to do any good cooking and good eating in one's own kitchen and dining room. The sermon without any concrete illustrations can be a crashing bore!

But we do also need abstractions in our lives. A cartoon shows a woman saying to the preacher after the service, "Your illustrations needed a sermon!" We need a friend to listen to our frustration in parenting, but we also need that friend or someone to help us analyze and investigate, for example, various *theories* of how to motivate children to do their homework. Some parents give financial rewards for good grades. Some parents allow their children to fail and experience the natural consequences of their failure as a way of motivating good study or work habits. Is it my job as a parent to do the homework with my child or simply to create conditions conducive to studying in the home? To analyze various abstract, theoretical approaches to the task of raising children can have invaluable, concrete results.

Much of the language in the New Testament epistles is abstract. Some have even criticized St. Paul for taking the simple, concrete religion *of* Jesus and turning it into a complex, abstract religion *about* Jesus. To some degree it is fair to say that while St. Paul gives us an abstract analysis of the theology of grace, Jesus lived the theology of grace in his daily activities, in concrete situations. He accepted sinners and ate with them. He associated with outcasts. The important thing to realize is that while abstract ideas and concrete actions are indeed quite different — in fact they are *opposites* — both are affirmed in the New Testament, and affirmed by both Jesus and Paul! Jesus told parables to illustrate his message: he gave concrete examples. Yet at the same time he admitted that some parables hid more than they revealed. He realized that many would take his parables or miracles in the wrong way and miss the point — the *abstract,* the *spiritual* point. There were also occasions when he had to explain the parables privately to the disciples. At other times he lamented how the people "hear without hearing." Jesus struggled with the *relationship* between concrete and abstract, this-worldly religion and other-worldly religion, the social dimensions of the gospel and the transcendent dimensions of the gospel.

3. Symbols are concrete abstractions

We have been talking about Surprising Symbols for the last few weeks, and now it is time to take note of the paradoxical nature of all our Christian symbols. All of these symbols are *concrete abstractions.* I think especially of the "spiritual body" that St. Paul describes in 1 Corinthians 15. *If* we understood the resurrection in overly concrete terms, we would speak of the resurrection of the *flesh.* The expression "spiritual body" means "a non-bodily body." It affirms both the concrete and the abstract. Paul is not being inconsistent by saying that "flesh and blood cannot inherit the Kingdom of God" and then in the same breath speaking of the "resurrection of the body." *Body* ("soma" in Greek) is a less concrete term than *flesh* ("sarx" in Greek). The paradox of the "*spiritual* body" is a concrete abstraction. Christian symbols move constantly back and forth between heaven and earth, between eternity and time, between spiritual and material, abstract and concrete. The purpose of a symbol is precisely to bridge the gap between the concrete and the abstract. The "spiritual body" is a perfect example. The cross is also a concrete abstraction, a symbol which has a meaning beyond what meets the eye. As a concrete reality, the cross of Christ is important in its own right, but it has also been chosen to represent a larger, unfathomable, abstract whole which we cannot fully express or understand. Jesus could speak only in parables and figures of speech of "the Kingdom of God" and we can speak of Jesus likewise only in symbols which, like parables, move back and forth between the opposite poles of concrete and abstract.

The artist, the poet, the mathematician, the musician, the theologian — all use their own particular kind of symbols to comprehend the whole of reality. All of them are caught between wanting to emphasize how much their symbols *do* say, and wanting to emphasize how much their symbols *do not* say. In other words, they want both to give us the "big picture" and yet at the same time show that the big picture is bigger than we can imagine!

We often speak of the importance of being "Christ-centered." The grace of God shown us in Christ is a concrete reality and we must be Christ-centered. But if we understand Christ and grace in nothing but a concrete way, we make a mistake. Then we become Christ-centered in the wrong way. We make Christ into little more than a magic lucky charm, a simple concrete "thing" that one must "have" in order to be saved. We forget that although the name Jesus is the specific name of a particular, "concrete" person, this name is also a symbol and it means "God saves," it means that we cannot put narrow, specific doctrinal or other limits on who God can save!

"Christ-centeredness" must not become an excuse for narrow-minded bigotry, a sophisticated form of holier-than-thou self-righteousness. "Christ" must be understood as an abstract symbol because not to do so is to deny the transcendent, divine nature of God's saving activity. When we look at Jesus we may see as much of God as we need to see, but not all that there is to see! Even though we say that the Christ, the Messiah, the "Anointed One" *has come,* our faith also includes a "not yet" dimension. We have not captured Christ like a bird in a cage!

In other words, *Christ* must be understood in both concrete and abstract ways. *Christ* is a *symbol* — a concrete abstraction — both amazingly simple and amazingly complex. To overdo the concrete side is to be Christ-centered in the wrong way. Overly concrete Christ-centeredness twists Jesus into the shape of a "personal automated pearly-gates access card." To overdo the abstract side is to be grace-centered in the wrong way. Overly abstract grace-centeredness waters down the gospel into pious platitudes.

Conclusion

Some realities are too great to be summed up in simple analogies or illustrations. Christian symbols transcend the distinction between concrete and abstract. Jesus simplified all the laws by choosing (“abstracting”) the “law of love,” and yet love is the most complex and demanding standard one could possibly follow. Christian symbols are as simple as a baby in a manger, and yet they are profound beyond words.

The Earthquakes That Put Things In Order

Introduction

It is not easy to keep a marriage and family together! Most married couples struggle through many upheavals. Some struggle and manage to stay together. Some struggle and eventually divorce. Equally as important as the *outcome* of the struggle is the *quality* of the struggle. Certainly, when we hold our marriages and our commitments together we deserve support and recognition for the effort we are making. But couples who stay together are not *automatically better* than those who do not manage to stay together. We do a great disservice if we don't applaud those couples who struggle to stay together. But we add insult to injury by looking askance at all divorce regardless of the circumstances. People who struggle through to a divorce may well have worked just as hard as — or harder than — couples who stay together. They have experienced great pain. Unthinking, wholesale comdemnation of divorce often amounts to kicking them when they are down!

Divorce can be, of course, an unwise, irresponsible, lazy attempt to escape from commitments. But in some cases, divorce may be the right decision, a positive step toward a new and better life for all concerned. To put it simply, a divorce *can be* a good thing.

1. An Earthquake Can Be Good

We see in our story for today that, surprising as it may seem, an *earthquake* can be a good thing! In fact, although the fifteen or so references to earthquakes in the Bible usually have somber overtones, the outcome of an earthquake story or reference is almost always positive. Elijah does not hear the voice of God in the great earthquake but in the "still, small voice." The earthquake is not, however, a villain in that story and the point is that God works in unexpected ways. Elsewhere in the Bible the earthquake is often pictured as God's way of shaking people up so that they will reevaluate their lives.

Luke's other earthquake story, in addition to this one in Acts, echos a point made in both Matthew and Mark: when there are "great earthquakes . . .signs in sun, moon and stars . . . perplexity at the roaring of the sea and the waves . . . the powers of the heavens . . . shaken . . . Now when these things begin to take place, look up and raise your heads, because your redemption is drawing near." (Luke chapter 21) The earthquake and the "heaven-quake" are seen as pointing to something positive!

In Matthew chapter 27 we read, "The earth shook, and the rocks were split; the tombs also were opened, and many bodies of the saints who had fallen asleep were raised, and . . . when the centurion and those who were with him, keeping watch over Jesus, saw the earthquake and what took place, they were filled with awe, and said, 'Truly this was the Son of God!' " Then again in chapter 28 the Gospel of Matthew pictures the resurrection of Jesus himself as being accompanied by an earthquake: "And behold, there was a great earthquake; for an angel of the Lord descended from heaven and came and rolled back the stone, and sat upon it."

In our text for today we encounter an earthquake that is a positive force in more ways than one. First, it shows the power of God to break down the strongest prison walls and to break open the shackles of Paul and Silas. The obvious message in this part of the story is that nothing can restrain the good news of the gospel. On the second level, the message of the story is that the apostles are not simply free *to escape;* they are free for the more positive purpose of sharing the good news! The apostles are not just free *from* something; they are free *for* something. They are free *for* witnessing to the love and grace of God in Jesus, the Christ. The jailer is so moved by the apostles' sense of inner freedom as evidenced by their not escaping when they could have escaped, that he too wants to share in this marvelous kind of freedom and love.

It is more than clear from these references that an earthquake can be a good thing. To use a contemporary expression, Jesus was a "mover and a shaker." Mixing metaphors a little, we can say that Jesus did not hesitate to "rock the boat." His followers preached a revolutionary message of grace, love, forgiveness, peace and hope. That message may shake us up, but it can also put things in order. We usually think of an earthquake as making a mess, as causing destruction. Like a divorce, an earthquake can be negative and destructive. But, like divorce, earthquakes can also help us to put our lives back in order, to clarify our goals and priorities, to get a new lease on life, to shake off old ways of looking at things, to open up and gain new vistas of freedom, love and faith. We do not escape from our responsibilities, but we find different and better ways of dealing with our responsibilities. So, finally today, we see *the earthquake* as one of the surprising symbols of Easter!

In California you will often see bumper stickers proclaiming, "This Is Earthquake Country!" Many Californians have learned to live with risk in a good sense, I believe. Every area of the world has its own kinds of risks — tornadoes, hurricanes, monsoons, scorching heat, or freezing cold. It would be unrealistic to try to find some place to live in the world where there was no possibility of a natural disaster. Even if there were such a place, such a "Shangri-La," if everybody on earth rushed to get there it wouldn't remain "Shangri-La" for long. The "population explosion" would itself be a natural disaster! Instead of spending our lives running away from risks, trying to avoid being shaken up, let us learn to celebrate the earthquake as one of the Surprising Symbols of Easter. Let us learn that to embrace life is to affirm a certain amount of openness to risk and change, to affirm a dynamic and not a static vision of our future in God.

2. A good shake-up can put things in order

One of the things that Paul and Silas shook up in the city of Philippi was the "religion business." The owners of a slave girl, whose supposed ability at "divination" (foretelling the future) was making them a lot of money, dragged Paul and Silas before the town magistrates after Paul and Silas had "put a hole in their drum" by curing her. They pretended that the apostles were "disturbing the peace," when actually their real motive for accusing Paul and Silas was simply a selfish, economic one. The apostles had hurt their business, and what was bad for business was bad for the city! Muhammed learned the same lesson when he criticized the religious tourist trade in Mecca, trade built around all the shrines and idols connected with the central shrine of the Black Stone. The people of Mecca thought him a troublemaker and tried to kill him. Jesus, too, threw the traders out of the temple, angrily reminding everyone that it was to be "a house of prayer."

Almost nothing seems to be in such consistent need of being shaken up as our priorities in the areas of money and economics. Ralph Waldo Emerson's famous line haunts us: "*Things* are in the saddle and ride mankind!" In our culture the problem may best be described as "consumerism." As Arthur McGill said, we think we must *have* everything we need to meet every contingency: we are petrified of finding ourselves needy. Other critics point out that we treat everything — art, education, music, religion, even people — as things to be consumed.

Instead of sharing our life with someone, we act as though a relationship with another person were a matter of exchanging "personality packages" and hoping that we get a fair exchange. By purchasing medical, social and other services we hope to remove all pain from our lives, not realizing that to some degree pain is a part of growth, and that if we are unable to feel sorrow we will also not be able to feel joy. Jesus shakes us up when he says, "Where your treasure is, there will your heart be also." He wants us to see, as Richard Wagner also tries to show in his famous *Ring* cycle of operas, that there is much in life that is far more important than power, money, and things. Love and sharing are more important. To the degree that we care about economic and material necessities, let us be concerned first and foremost that the fruits of the earth be justly distributed among all of God's children. Let us learn to be producers as well as consumers; in other words, let us constantly remind ourselves that while it is important to affirm our neediness and to be ready to receive, it is also in some ways "*better to give* than to receive."

In his book *Turning East,* Harvey Cox provides an analysis of our Western fascination with the religions of India and China. He devotes one chapter to a discussion of the relationship between Eastern forms of *meditation* and the biblical practice of the *sabbath.* He notes a strong similarity between Eastern meditation, and the sabbath concept of setting aside special time when the accent is on *being* rather than *doing*. But then he also takes note of a striking irony. The Eastern practitioners of meditation have come to the West to help us become less materialistic, less enamored with the *things* in this world of illusion. But in the process, they themselves have often become rich. This somewhat cynical insight should shake us up, and remind us that it takes constant vigilance to keep our priorities in order.

The businessmen in our text were exploiting a poor slave for their own material advantage. The preachers of the gospel of Jesus freed her from this exploitation. Ultimately, the gospel leads to freedom from all forms of slavery! The gospel ultimately shook the institution of slavery to its foundations and it continues to "shake down" all forms of exploitation. The gospel creates an earthquake that puts things in order.

Another outstanding example of how a good shake-up can put things in order can be found in the life and writings of Pastor Dietrich Bonhoeffer, executed by the Nazis for his opposition to the Hitler regime. By his prayerful decision to participate in the plot to kill Hitler, Bonhoeffer provided us with a model that shakes us out of our business-as-usual ruts. In his writings, collected by his friend Eberhard Bethge, some of which are included under the simple title *Ethics,* Bonhoeffer begins with the surprising observation that our "knowledge of good and evil" is *not* a point in our favor. He writes, "The knowledge of good and evil signifies the complete reversal of man's knowledge, which hitherto had been solely knowledge of God as his origin. In knowing good and evil he knows what only the origin, God Himself, can know and ought to know."*

Bonhoeffer goes on to show how supposedly sophisticated ethical decisions and judgments tend to deny the freedom and simplicity of "doing the will of God." Our sinfulness consists not so much in making faulty ethical decisions, but in *judging* other people as to whether *they* are good or evil. Jesus comes not to condemn but to save. To be justified by God's grace means that when we endeavor to do God's will we can leave it up to God to defend our decisions and actions. We can act in love and let it go at that. It is God who justifies.

Bonhoeffer's earthshaking discovery was that in the decisive moment, the act of putting the bomb in the briefcase next to Hitler was simply the right thing to do. He was *not judging* Hitler. He was

---

*(Macmillan Co., NY, 1955)

trying to save the lives of children who were being sent into hopeless battles, and an entire race condemned to the gas chambers. Bonhoeffer's *Ethics* disturbs us by calling in question our moralistic nitpicking. He shakes us up by suggesting that it can be precisely our "moral sense," our penchant for *judgmentalism,* that is our greatest failing, our greatest sin. In this he reminds us of the words of Oscar Wilde: "I never came across anyone in whom the moral sense was dominant who was not heartless, cruel, vindictive, log stupid and entirely lacking in the smallest sense of humanity." The history of the persecution of the early church by the Romans in the name of their devotion to Caesar reminds us that there is a thin line between conviction and bigotry, between faith and fanaticism. If the words and warnings of Bonhoeffer and Wilde make the earth move under our feet, perhaps that will be good for us!

Conclusion

A good conductor always keeps the musicians a little "shook up" — sometimes with humor, and sometimes with serious criticism and instruction — always trying to keep the ensemble on its toes. Once upon a time, a few years back, Robert Fountain, who had made his reputation as a great conductor at Oberlin College in Ohio, was rehearsing the University of Wisconsin Choral Union for a performance of Handel's Oratorio, *Israel in Egypt.* The piece is a sort of musical version of the ten plagues and the escape through the Red Sea. At one point in the rehearsal Dr. Fountain suddenly stopped and said, in his usual emphatic manner, "You know, I would love to give you all a grade of A for your efforts, but I'm afraid that at this point all I can give you is *a big red C!"* Some were slower to catch the pun than others, but generally his clever ploys to keep everyone motivated and growing were remarkably effective. Since music and theology are by all accounts closely related, perhaps it would not be too far afield to put an "Amen" to this series by using the Surprising Symbol of *God* as the ultimate, gracious, yet awe-inspiring conductor who regularly shakes us up, but who also helps us all to make beautiful music together.

www.ingramcontent.com/pod-product-compliance
Lightning Source LLC
LaVergne TN
LVHW020647100826
845148LV00012B/2361

* 9 7 8 0 8 9 5 3 6 7 5 1 8 *